YOU CALL THIS A
FAMILY?

Campus Life Books

Against All Odds
Alive: Daily Devotions
Alive II: Daily Devotions
The Campus Life Guide to Dating
The Campus Life Guide to Making and Keeping Friends
The Campus Life Guide to Surviving High School
The Life of the Party: A True Story of Teenage Alcoholism
The Lighter Side of Campus Life
A Love Story: Questions and Answers on Sex
Peer Pressure: Making It Work for You
What Teenagers Are Saying about Drugs and Alcohol
Worth the Wait: Love, Sex, and Keeping the Dream Alive
You Call This a Family? Making Yours Better

YOU CALL THIS A
FAMILY?

MAKING YOURS BETTER

GREGG LEWIS & TIM STAFFORD

A DIVISION OF CTi
CampusLife
BOOKS

ZondervanPublishingHouse
Grand Rapids, Michigan
A Division of HarperCollins*Publishers*

You Call This a Family?
Copyright © 1990 by Campus Life Books
First printing, April 1986

Published by
Zondervan Publishing House
1415 Lake Drive, S.E.,
Grand Rapids, Michigan 49506.

Library of Congress Cataloging-in-Publication Data

You call this a family? / Gregg Lewis and Tim Stafford.
   p. cm.
  Reprint. Originally published: 1986.
  Summary: Presents advice to Christian teens on how to understand
and improve family life and develop closer parent-child
relationships.
   ISBN 0-310-71091-X
  1. Parent and child—United States—Case studies. 2. Family—
United States—Religious life—Case studies. [1. Parent and
child. 2. Family life. 3. Christian life.] I. Lewis, Gregg A.
II. Stafford, Tim.
HQ755.85.Y68   1990
306.874—dc20   90–41247
                                               CIP
                                              AC

The article "Mom, I've Outgrown You" by Ann R. Eddy is reprinted with
permission from the May 1972 *Redbook Magazine*. Copyright © 1972 by the
Hearst Corporation.

The article "The Day Mom Cried" by Gerald Moore is reprinted with permission
from the September 1980 *Reader's Digest*. Copyright © 1980 by The Reader's
Digest Assn., Inc.

The article "Lost to Each Other" by Sue Monk Kidd originally appeared in the
June 1979 *Guideposts* magazine under the title "Don't Let It End This Way." It is
reprinted with permission. Copyright © 1979 by Guideposts Associates, Inc.

Some of the material in this book has been adapted from *The Trouble With
Parents,* copyright © 1979, Zondervan.

Printed in the United States of America

90 91 92 93 94 / CH / 5 4 3 2 1

CONTENTS

About the YOUTHSOURCE™ Publishing Group

YOUTHSOURCE™ books, tapes, videos, and other resources pool the expertise of three of the finest youth-ministry resource providers in the world:

Campus Life Books—publishers of the award-winning *Campus Life* magazine, who for nearly fifty years have helped high schoolers live Christian lives.

Youth Specialties—serving ministers to middle-school, junior-high, and high-school youth for over twenty years through books, magazines, and training events such as the National Youth Workers Convention.

Zondervan Publishing House—one of the oldest, largest, and most respected evangelical Christian publishers in the world.

Campus Life	**Youth Specialties**	**Zondervan**
465 Gundersen Dr.	1224 Greenfield Dr.	1415 Lake Dr., S.E.
Carol Stream, IL 60188	El Cajon, CA 92021	Grand Rapids, MI 49506
708/260-6200	619/440-2333	616/698-6900

Introduction

What's your family like? Where would you rate it on a scale of one to ten if one meant "most happy" and ten meant "most unhappy"?

In a recent survey conducted by *Campus Life* magazine, the majority of our readers said they felt very good about their families. No one convinced us his or her family could be called perfect, but most respondents weren't about to trade in theirs for an unknown model.

If reader feedback is so positive, why then does *Campus Life* magazine print so many stories about families with problems? Why write a book like this about families and family problems?

First, there will never be a more significant influence in your life than your relationship with your family. You may argue, "What about my relationship with God? Or with my future mate?" It's true: These and other relationships can greatly change and mold you. And certainly you make a lot of your own choices and you can create your own role in life. But if your life were a script and someone made a movie of it, your family would get most of the screen credits for writing it. The core that is you, the person you start as, is determined most of all by your family.

Second, we're publishing this book because every family could be better. Even those who responded to our survey saying they lived in a happy family pointed out specific problems they wished could be resolved. Many thousands of other young people live in desperately unhappy families. We believe this book can help both the unhappy and the happy.

If you've thumbed through the book, you've seen it's made up of many short chapters by different authors. Many books on families begin with a verbal blueprint of what a family should be like. Then they offer advice on how yours can fit the model. They have one author, one perspective, one blueprint for all families.

We don't think that's quite fair. Every family, happy or unhappy, is different, with diverse problems and needs. And that's why this book has a number of writers who, though their views don't conflict, each offer thought-provoking viewpoints, personal stories, and models of families they've seen working and failing.

This book contains a wealth of information. But it will not spell out for you exactly how to get along with your family. Rather you will have to think about how each chapter applies, or fails to apply, to your situation. You'll find yourself, we hope, going back to some of the articles to read them over. We hope you'll also frequently find yourself putting down the book just to look into space and think.

For there's one statement that does fairly apply to all families: They matter. They matter to you; they matter to us; and they matter even more to God, who thought them up. For all these reasons, we've put together this book. We hope the ideas and insights will prod you to action and enable you to help make your family better.

Gregg Lewis
for the editors of *Campus Life*

WHAT'S THE TROUBLE?

It can be mystifying. Having lived all your life with these people, you've grown to be much like them. You eat the same food. You probably agree on most TV shows. If they are nervous, you probably are too—your personality has developed so as to be similar to theirs. You even look like them. And for most of your life you probably got along pretty well.

Yet sometimes they seem to squelch the life out of you. It's like they never want you to grow up. Can't they see you are able to take care of yourself? Why do they insist on all those rules?

Why do they have such an ability to drive you crazy? Why is it you can't shrug off their opinions, their remarks? Where did all this trouble and tension come from?

Your parents ask similar questions. Did they do something wrong? Or do they have a kid who's abnormal?

The first step in understanding the trouble you have with your parents (whether it's constant or occasional) is to realize a lot of changes are taking place—both in and around your family. And as these first chapters point out, transitions almost always cause tension and trouble.

THE WAR OF INDEPENDENCE
Penny Smith, M.D.

W e psychiatrists see an unusual side of life, and often the problems are exaggerated. Some kids who come to see me blurt out feelings that they have never told to anyone else. Others are so scared and shy at first that I can't get them to say a complete sentence. It's pretty rare for a teenager to come to me on his own. Usually Mom or Dad has encouraged him, which automatically puts two strikes against me.

I see a variety of problems in teenagers, but almost all have one thing in common. They're all bloody, bandaged victims of the "War of Independence." That war is a conflict required of just about everyone who grows up, and usually it's waged against the parent.

The battlefields change over the years. Now it's things like drugs and sexuality, whereas at another time hair length or skirt length set the grounds of conflict.

When I can bring a teenager to the place where he opens up, he usually says something like this: "Is there *any* way you can get my mom and dad to understand?" He's almost pleading. There's a brick wall ten feet thick between him and his parents.

Unfortunately, I usually must reply, "Probably not. I doubt they'll ever understand." Parents have simply forgotten what it was like when they went through the War of Independence.

It's too bad we have to use analogies like war to describe the process. It's really a natural growth process. Every person has to go through a stretching, expanding period when he finds his own identity, apart from his parents.

An infant's life is totally dependent on his parents. Even

through grade school and junior high, most of a kid's life is determined for him by others: teachers, parents, youth directors. They set rules for him, tell him what he should learn and believe, what decisions he should make. But suddenly, in a brief period, the kid has to prepare himself to make all his own decisions and find out who he is and what he wants to be. No wonder the battlefield gets a little smoky sometimes.

It's interesting that the Bible records only one event from Jesus' growing-up years. He was twelve years old and had gone to the temple with his parents. His mother and father took off on the journey home, assuming Jesus was with them, but suddenly they found that he was missing. Frightened, and probably angry, they rushed back to the temple and saw Jesus calmly holding court with the scholars. Can't you just imagine Mary's anxiety? "Son, do you realize what you put me through? I was worried sick!"

Note Jesus' reaction. He didn't sulk or throw a tantrum. He obeyed his parents and went with them. Jesus understood the War of Independence. He knew his parents would have to adjust to a new scene as he grew up, and he could handle their overworried reaction.

By the time you're a teenager, your parents have been looking after you for thirteen years. You can't expect them to let go of those strings overnight. It takes time and understanding, from both parties.

Psychologists who study teenagers are finding out there are vast differences between the ways teenagers and adults think and respond. The teenager's brain undergoes dramatic changes. He begins to use his brain for what scientists call "formal operation." For the first time he can logically manipulate thought and therefore, quite naturally, the teenager spends a lot of time inside his own head—thinking, figuring things out.

Parents see their kid as spacy and lazy. But you have to understand where the parents are coming from. They are concerned with survival. What's on your dad's mind on any given day? His job satisfaction, rising prices, insurance bills, plans for your college, tensions with your mother. Your mother is probably concerned with feeding you, raising your brothers and sisters, taking care of relatives. If she works, her task is doubly complex.

Moreover, most parents are plain scared. They didn't have drug trafficking in their schools when they were growing up, but they read in *Time* magazine about drugs on school campuses—even in grade schools. They read the statistics of kids who have sex and of the hundreds of thousands of unwed mothers, and they're scared to death about you.

These are some of the reasons I say, "No, I can't cross that communication barrier between you and your parents." I don't think there can be perfect, clear understanding between parents and teenagers. You're coming from two different sets of pressures and tensions.

So, if you feel your parents don't understand you—relax. Join the millions. You probably don't understand your parents either.

Your parents *will* fail you. That's a revolutionary thought to most kids. Often the most rebellious kids, who really hurt their parents, are plagued with tremendous guilt feelings. It's been hammered into them all their life that their parents are always right, and when differences erupt they feel it's their fault. More probably, the problem belongs to all of you.

Is the situation hopeless? I've seen too many happy families to believe that. I think the biggest lesson a kid can learn is to accept and care for his parents even when there is no communication. Too often when problems arise, the teenager sulks or refuses to talk or won't cooperate around the house. Maybe he starts acting deliberately rebellious, antagonizing his parents. That's a dead end. My advice is to keep on trying to be understanding even when you're not getting through to your parents.

The most important ingredient to successful families is unconditional love. A parent should communicate to his kids that he loves and accepts them *regardless*. Fill in anything you want—the kid can run away, reject everything the parent stands for—but the teenager has to believe his parents will love him no matter what. Jesus' parable of the prodigal son, as told in Luke 15, is the best example.

Only in the family can you find that kind of love. James

Dobson describes in his book *Hide or Seek* how you rate in our society. He says society gives you a gold coin of self-respect if you're beautiful. You get a silver coin if you have a lot of brains. And you get a bronze coin of self-respect for having money. The family should be directly opposed to that sort of value rating. You are valuable because you were born. You belong to your family simply because you exist. And no matter how irritating you think your situation is, it's unlikely you'll find any other group in society that genuinely accepts you as freely as your family accepts you. If your parents are wise enough to love you in spite of anything and everything, you stand a chance of surviving the War of Independence without wounds.

You too have a responsibility. When did you last express interest in your dad's job or in your parents' friends? When did you last ask about their hobbies or the vacations they took before you came along? Kids can hold the key to their parents' sense of self-worth. Parents have invested an awful lot in you— are they seeing any return on their investment?

Your most important job is this: You must love and accept your parents no matter what. No matter how boorish or unjust or cruel they appear to you, if you respond with love and maturity, God will honor that response.

McPHERSON

Getting a date with Ellen Zeffler was more difficult than Walt had expected.

The Changing Family

Verne Becker

Lots of people today lament the "breakdown of the family." But just what is the family "breaking down" from? How has the family changed since the beginning of the century?

What you're about to read is more than a history lesson; it's an explanation, at least in part, of the conflicts and tensions you may be feeling in your family. The next time you storm into your room and slam the door in frustration, remember that millions of other families are experiencing similar upheaval.

Then: *Most families lived on farms.* Only 30 percent lived in urban or metropolitan areas. People were accustomed to building their own houses and barns, growing their own food, raising their own animals. Families often lived in the same house all their lives.

> **Now:** *Most families live in urban or suburban areas.* The figures have reversed. Fewer than 30 percent of the population live in rural settings. And less than 5 percent are farmers. Families must depend more on outside sources for food, clothing, even jobs.

Then: *Mom stayed home and canned vegetables.* While Dad spent his days farming the land, Mom logged in hours of cooking (from scratch), cleaning (on hands and knees), and washing or making clothes (by hand).

> **Now:** *Mom is more likely to hold an outside job.* In 1950, 18.4 percent of U.S. mothers had full-time jobs outside the home. Now nearly 60 percent work full time.

"I interrupt this program for a special announcement: Get out there and mow the lawn, David!"

Then: *Primitive machines and methods made ordinary tasks difficult and time-consuming.* Mom *needed* to be home all day because household tasks actually took all day. Cooking, canning, cleaning, sewing, and mending could easily consume every waking hour—particularly when Mom had no refrigerator, washing machine, or vacuum cleaner.

> **Now:** *Technology has reduced or eliminated many household tasks.* Prepared foods can be refrigerated or frozen and heated up in the microwave. It's often a better use of Mom's time

and money to buy factory-made clothes than to make them—although she can make them much more quickly now than before. Automatic washers and dryers can be operated by anyone, and permanent-press fabrics make ironing less of a chore. The effect of all these technological advances is to eliminate many of the roles traditionally assigned to Mom. And today many women are searching for meaning in other roles.

Then: *Children helped pay the family bills.* By working on the farm and helping with the chores, thereby reducing the need to hire additional labor, kids actually made money for the family. One researcher estimated that a teenager was worth $5,000 a year in income for the average farmer at the turn of the century.

Now: *Children drive families into debt.* Kids don't help with the farm anymore, because the family farms have all but disappeared. Instead, a recent study estimates that by the time you're eighteen, your parents will have spent more than $82,000 on you. And if *you* were to have a child today, the U.S. Department of Agriculture figures it would cost about $141,000 to raise him to age eighteen.

Then: *Families had more kids.* Since kids were economic assets, people made sure to have plenty of them. Four or five kids were common, and six or seven hardly raised an eyebrow. With such large families, children didn't receive as much individual attention and they quickly learned to submit to the needs of a larger group. Dinner was at 6:00—be there or starve.

Now: *Families make fewer babies.* The national average is now less than two children per family. And as families get smaller, the dynamics change. It's easier for you to get special treatment. If you have play rehearsal after school, Mom'll reheat your dinner later on.

Then: *Dad ruled the family*. Probably the main reason is that he was home all day, and society's lines of authority were clearly drawn. Fatherly rule didn't always work—some fathers were cruel and insensitive—but everyone knew who was boss.

Now: *Just who runs the family isn't clear.* Tony Campolo has gone so far as to say that today *kids run many families*. He argues that with Dad being away at work more, he is less able to maintain discipline at home. Mom acts much less as an authoritarian and more as an agent of love and nurture. This encourages the kids to push harder for their demands. As a result, families often plan their schedules around the kids' activities and needs. More than half of the country's gross national product is spent on or by kids under twenty.

Then: *Marriage was an economic necessity.* A man had to marry if he wanted a farm of his own. He needed his wife to cook and keep house while he worked from morning till night in the fields. And he also needed her to raise his kids so they could help with the harvest. Women needed marriage, too, since they rarely learned wage-earning skills.

Now: *People marry for emotional reasons.* In today's techno-industrial society, single men and women can find jobs and support themselves without rushing into marriage. In short, marriage isn't *economically* necessary. Several shifts in marriage patterns have resulted:

First, people are waiting longer to marry.

Second, more young men and women are living independently of their parents, in contrast to earlier days when kids lived at home until they got married.

Third, more unmarried couples are living together. Between 1970 and 1983, the number tripled. They now comprise 4 percent of all American "couple-households."

Then: *Divorces were infrequent and frowned upon.* Financial dependence on one's spouse had a way of keeping couples together, even if they were unhappy. Marriage was as much an economic contract as a social/spiritual one. And when couples did divorce, society's stigma made them wish they hadn't.

Now: *Divorce is commonplace.* The latest tally predicts that half of all recent first marriages will end in divorce. One out of three white kids and two of three black kids born in the late 1970s will watch their parents' marriage break up before the kids reach sixteen.

Then: *The only single parents were widows or widowers.* In colonial America, the high mortality rate resulted in most marriages lasting less than ten years. Death was the only thing that broke up families. And when it did, the surviving spouse quickly remarried.

Now: *Single-parent families are increasing, largely because of high divorce rates and out-of-wedlock births.* In 1950, 9.4 percent of all families were supported solely by women. Last year the figure had grown to 16 percent. Since single moms must usually find a job and pay for day care for their children, they often endure financial hardship. According to the Census Bureau, more than three million single-parent families lived in poverty in 1983. Most of these trends, you can see, work to break down family unity and cohesion.

Is there any hope for the family, with all these changing forces in our society? And what do these broad societal trends have to do with the little group of people you will eat dinner with tonight? At *Campus Life* we believe a positive answer to the first question depends a lot on practical answers to the second. If social trends are tearing families apart, we will have to counteract those trends in our own homes.

What do all the changes in society have to do with the daily hassles you may have with your parents over practical things such as cars, clothes, and curfew? The connection isn't always clear or direct. But if you understand some of the bigger picture, the broader pressures, you'll realize that your difficulties aren't simply the result of your own or your parents' personal failings. Some problems are bigger than you (or your parents) are.

These realizations may help you keep from placing all the blame for your family's troubles on your parents or on yourself. We hope they'll encourage you to work *with* your parents, instead of against them, to make your family better.

UNDER-STANDING PARENTS

You know how you feel. But as you grew up your parents were always those Big People who knew everything and told you what to do. It's hard to imagine them being scared, getting their feelings hurt, feeling shy trying to talk to you, or worrying about what you think of them. But they do. And they get upset, just as you do, about how hard it can be to get along.

They love you. Though they may have a funny way of showing it, most parents do love their kids and are constantly telling them so. It's just that they sometimes use a unique language of love that you need to learn to understand.

That's what this next section is about: Understanding. Once you begin to understand the fears and feelings of your parents, once you can imagine how life seems to them right now, you can start to look intelligently for ways to make your family better.

Why Are Your Parents Scared?

Tim Stafford

They have been taught (as they taught you) not to show fear. Instead, they nag you or act tough. But at heart's center they are afraid. You scare them. Why?

They are scared because you are getting away from them.

They wanted you in the first place, and in their planning you would be their baby. You lived up to that at first. No matter how often you were a crying pain, you were theirs. You needed them. They cuddled you, encircled you with their arms, and thought you were a little doll.

Now you're shattering their conception. You point out what they would rather forget: they chose you but you never chose them. You may love them (they hope you do), but you don't belong to them. You are getting away; and though they may know better, they fear they soon will be left behind.

They are scared that you won't make up for their failures.

By now they know that some things they wanted to do will never be done. They will never be famous. They will never be comfortably rich.

They will never again be good-looking. They will die unmarked, part of a list in the newspaper, one of a few thousand who died that day.

And by now they have transferred their hopes to you. Why do you think they care how you look? Why do you think they care what grades you get, or about your friends?

They want you to do for yourself what they will never be able to do for themselves. And they're scared you won't.

They are scared because they know how easy it is to waste your life.

They know, by experience, that there are three wrong directions for every one that's right. Half their friends are unhappy. Are they, too? They don't want that for you.

But they know how easily life slips away through a casual decision to stick with the wrong friends, wrong habits, or wrong thinking.

So they are scared, and they worry.

All right, you're stronger than they think. You're confident, but they're afraid. You know where you're going, and they're not so sure. You don't have to absorb their fear, but can you respect it?

They are scared because they feel powerless.

You may sometimes feel your parents control your life. But your parents often feel helpless because they realize how little control they actually have. When you were a child they could command you. Now they have to try to influence you. The shift in your relationship makes them uneasy. They see all the dangerous things going on in the world, all the changes that have taken place since they were teenagers, and yet they know they need to gradually give you more and more freedom. They realize they are sending you out into a world full of potential dangers and they know they can't protect you. It frightens them.

They are scared because they can't talk to you.

They love you, and that love forms words that stick to their tongues. They want to share the stories of their lives with you, but they are tales from another time about aunts and uncles you never knew. And you don't laugh at their jokes.

They want to tell you what you mean to them, but they're embarrassed and you're busy doing homework.

They want to give you good advice, but the TV is on and who can talk?

They're afraid that you, the one they love, have left them behind and they won't be able to talk to you again. They want to talk, but how?

They are scared because they feel insecure as parents.

They didn't learn parenting in college or graduate school. No one ever taught your mom and dad how to be good parents. If they were fortunate, their own parents set a good example for them to learn from. But times, circumstances, and people change. And what worked a generation ago doesn't always apply today.

At best, parenting is a trial and error job. Most parents realize they are going to make a lot of mistakes. They can only hope and pray the mistakes won't be too serious because the stakes, the lives of their children, are so high.

Basically, your parents are scared because they love you.

They don't want to fail as parents. But mostly they don't want to fail you. And they're afraid they will.

The Trouble with Parents

Philip Yancey

Both the students and parents were nervous. A suburban church had thrown them together for a weekend retreat. The kids banded together, defensive. So did the parents.

The first evening the two groups were separated. Parents went off to watch a film, while Campus Life Director Don Mardock stayed with the crowd of teenagers in a bare room with two oversized blackboards. "We're going to do something you may have wanted to do for a long time," he began. "For the next thirty minutes, I want you to come up with every gripe you can think of against your parents."

Kids once quiet and bored snapped to attention. A few smart-alecks tried to be clever: "My mother wants my room to look like a suite in the Waldorf Hotel," or "My dad hasn't been wrong about anything since second grade." But before long, the emotional tone had changed. Serious, pent-up tensions came out, and Don patiently wrote each one on the blackboard:

"My parents don't trust me."

"They never admit they're wrong."

"They don't listen."

"They want to live their lives through me."

When the half-hour ended, Don had completely filled the huge blackboard with more than forty major gripes.

Then Don rolled the blackboard against the wall, and the kids switched places with their parents upstairs. After explaining the procedure, Don was immediately deluged with the parents' gripes about their kids:

"Kids have no understanding of the pressures I go through."

"I live in the suburbs for *their* safety and they blame me for being racially prejudiced!"

"How can I trust my kids when they've done nothing to earn my trust?"

"My son's had three traffic tickets and two accidents, and he sulks when I don't give him the car."

"Mine are moody."

In a few minutes, Don had filled half of the second board, and hands were still popping up. He spotted one distraught-looking lady with her hand propped up. "Don," she began in an unsteady voice, "why are we enjoying this so much? Look at the things up there—pressure, irresponsibility, lack of trust, no communication. Who are we trying to fool? Those things are just as true of us as they are of our kids."

Silence. A few parents nodded agreement; others spoke out.

"She's right, Don. Our kids have problems, but they're not that different from ours. We're not perfect." After a lot of discussion, the parents asked Don to erase all twenty of the gripes they had so eagerly contributed. Instead, they wrote on the board a single sentence that summarized their one most important gripe.

After Don had wheeled that blackboard against the wall, the teenagers piled back into the same room and sat across from their parents. They were chattering, enthusiastic about the chance to charge their parents with whatever bugged them, no holds barred.

Don rolled out the black-board full of gripes against parents. He randomly asked kids in the group to explain. One by one, kids stood up and gave examples of how cold, unresponsive, and unreasonable their parents were. The parents sat in silence, listening to eloquent explanations of all forty gripes. Some kids were funny, some emotional, but everyone got across a pointed criticism.

Now for the parents. The kids were excited, spoiling for a fight, ready to blast whatever the parents had written. Don wheeled the board around. In large letters was written this one sentence: "The one thing we don't like about our kids is that they're too much like we are."

Total silence. A lot of thinking, tears, and one-on-one communication followed. It lasted far into the night.

BOOTS

Name Withheld

My father is yelling at me. Actually, he is yelling at my mother, but I'm the only one around so I get the onslaught. And I'm sick of it: sick of the bulging eyes, sick of the reddened face, sick of the unbridled anger.

He is a chameleon. One moment he peacefully flips through the paper, and the next he stomps around the house in a rage, pursuing his prey.

"Stop it, Dad! You're doing it again. You always come at me. I tell you I don't want to hear it, but you do it anyway!"

His yelling still rings in my ears as his rough, calloused hands fall to his side, and he looks at me apologetically. He slumps into a dining room chair with a sigh.

I stand over him, hands on hips. I am shaking my head, and in low tones I scold him as if he were a child. He knows he cannot control the beast within, and for a moment I see him question himself. His eyes reveal it; they are moist and dark, defeated. He is thinking, trying to rationalize his behavior to himself. After all, he is an engineer—he's supposed to analyze things. Part of his anger stems from the pile of unpaid bills in the kitchen. As his silent analysis continues, the image of my mother, his oppressor, comes to mind. She nags him endlessly about the family finances, and it brings the hardness to his eyes.

He turns to me, his defenses up. "I know, I know, but . . . but you've got to respect the fact that your mother is constantly hounding me to . . ." His voice is agitated; he is changing into the monster again.

But my voice rises above his, assured, final, and destructive.

"No, Dad, no, I have no respect for you. I have no respect, none anymore, none whatsoever . . . no respect whatsoever!"

I know what I am saying and I know that the assurance with which it is delivered is damaging, maybe crushing. I know my father; I know he holds the respect his sons have for him as his greatest treasure. I close the door behind me and rush upstairs without waiting to witness the effect of my words.

A while later I descend the stairs and flop down at the bottom, my feet sprawled in front of me. The heat of the furnace feels good, and an hour or two of reading has left me somewhat drained of emotion. Looking out the window, I notice it is overcast but bright outdoors; cold, yet inviting. I decide to go for a walk.

Mom says Dad has left on a walk of his own and that he said he didn't know when he'd be back.

"I respect your father for what he is and for his principles," she says, looking hard at me.

"I knew that was coming," I say, turning away from her. "I'm glad you respect him, because I don't anymore, and I hope he's hurt, I hope he's crushed . . . I hope he's decimated." I know deep down that I didn't really mean that. But I still want to hurt him; I owe him one.

Angrily, I tell Mom she's just as bad as Dad sometimes, in her own quiet, biting way. She starts to cry, but, since she knows I hate to see her cry, she holds back, just like she suppresses her feelings every day.

"I try, I really do," she pleads.

"Bull," I say. I feel like saying "bull" to anything Mom and Dad say for the rest of their lives. Why must I be an innocent bystander to their battle? But as I look at my mother sitting across from me at the dining room table, I realize she and Dad are waging more of a battle within themselves than with each other.

A minute later I sit in the living room lacing up my "new" boots. The other night Dad explained how his size 10½ boots really didn't fit him, and I had mentioned that my newer boots were 11's and too big on me. We thought about trading.

We sat there in our chairs, examining and comparing each other's boots in a childishly simple way, both reluctant to give up our own, yet both eager to own the other's. Finally my father suggested that we each try them out on a walk before we make the final decision. And that is what I am about to do.

I stride across the field, kicking up the light dusting of snow, getting the feel of "my" boots. Soon I am deep into the woods, winding my way between dense pines, skidding across icy banks, bushwacking my way to a frozen swamp where I hope to indulge in some shoeskating. I arrive, wheezing, my breath clouding my vision. But the swamp is dry; to my disappointment, the thin ice crunches under my feet. I trudge on in search of another spot to skate. Checking one possibility just past a nearby tree line, I find that it, too, is dry.

I gaze around. Things look different with the new snow: More open, more cold, and yet the woods enclose and comfort me as always. I am quickly forgetting my bitterness toward my father. If it's true that time is the great healer, then these woods are a sweet time warp.

Just a little farther away lies the beaver pond. I visit there often after school during the fall to watch the beavers and listen to the solitude. But today I discover bootsteps on the main trail. And I wonder who would come this way.

To my delight, I find the pond's surface to be hard and smooth. Throwing off my coat, I run out onto the ice and glide across its white-powdered expanse. Sometime later, I retrieve my coat and leave the pond, my legs still aching from the effort of trying to run without falling flat on my face.

The afternoon sun forces its way through a gray cloud layer, and its orange light breaks up as it penetrates the woods. I walk quickly, for the wind is now blowing in my face, stinging my ears. I rub them with my gloves and hardly notice the same bootsteps before me.

Suddenly it occurs to me whose bootsteps mark the path. This is where my father must have gone for his walk—in the woods, to the beaver pond, to be alone as I have.

The discovery catches me by surprise. Somehow I had pictured him stomping up the dirt road that runs past our house, his back haunched, head lowered. Instead, he too journeyed into the time warp, his eyes raised toward the tall pines, his weathered skin bracing against the cold. His fresh footprints haunt me.

I arrive home cold and hungry. My brother and his wife have come for dinner, which Mom is already preparing. I say hello to them and step into the foyer, marveling at how *very* cold it is outside. I hang up my coat and place my gloves on the wood rack to dry.

Sitting at the dining room table is my father, wearing a thick sweater. His skin is still red from the cold, like mine. I enter the dining room, not knowing whether to remain hostile.

He looks up at me and smiles warmly. "Did you try out my boots? Did they fit okay?"

I can't help but return the smile. "Yes, Dad, I did, and they worked out fine." I raise my leg, twisting my foot and admiring the boot's ruggedness.

"Yeah," he says, "I tried yours out too."

Treating a Friend Like a Father

Tim Stafford

I read somewhere that you should treat your parents with all the respect, patience, and understanding you would have toward your best friend.

"That is how I have always treated them," I said to myself. But when I thought about it, I wasn't so sure. I went on a brief daydream, wondering what it would be like if my best friend, Ernie Estabrook, came over, and . . .

"Hi," Ernie said. "Are you ready to go to the basketball game?"

"Would you get off my back?" I said in my most exasperated tone. "You're always rushing me. What difference does it make if we're a little late?"

Ernie shrugged. "None, I guess. What did you do this afternoon?"

"Nothing," I grunted.

"Did you have practice after school?"

"Nah."

"You came straight home?"

"Yeah."

"So what did you do?"

"Nothing!" I exploded. "Why do you always pry into my private life?"

"Sorry," Ernie said. He looked a little hurt and tried to change the subject. "Hey, I saw you talking to Charlotte. How do you rate? She's really something, isn't she?"

"Look, let's make an agreement," I said. "You let me make my own friendships, and I'll let you make yours. I'm mature enough to know who I want to be friends with and who I don't. I can't see that it's any of your business."

"Hey, I was just trying— aw, forget it. Let's go to the game."

"I'll be ready in a minute," I said. "Can I have five bucks?"

"Well, I don't know," Ernie said doubtfully. "I don't have much money. Don't you have any money of your own?"

"Where would I get it?" I asked sarcastically. "I suppose you want me to get a job on top of a full day at school and playing in the band."

"Who said anything about a job?"

"Everyone always wants you to get terrific grades and practically be an Einstein, but they won't lend you the money to go to a basketball game and relax once in a while. I suppose you'd prefer I went out drinking. That's cheaper, you know. It wouldn't cost you a cent."

"Forget I said anything," Ernie said. "You can have the money. Let's just go to the game. We're late already."

"You're *always* pushing me," I grumbled on the way out the door. But I stopped. "Ernie, do we have to go in that crummy car? It looks so *old*! Everyone else drives a new car, and I have to go in that beat-up refugee from a junkyard. Can't you get something new?"

"I would if I had the money," Ernie mumbled.

"That's the trouble with you," I said. "All you think about is money. You're always so worried about spending a little bit extra. You're so tied up in cash, you don't take time to think about more meaningful things."

"I guess you're right," Ernie said, his head down.

"You bet I'm right," I said. "And if you think I'm going to sit with you at the game, you're crazy!"

At this point in my day-dream my father walked into the room. I took my feet off the coffee table, sat up straight, and said, "Hi, Dad. How did your day go?"

"Now what do you want?" he sighed.

"No, you're supposed to say, 'Dad, the car's back safe and sound, and *in* the garage,' *not* 'Dad, how good is your insurance?' "

A RIPPING
OF FABRIC

Harold Myra

I was full of excitement as I stuffed my Datsun with suitcases, typewriter, and books. From a small town in the Pennsylvania mountains, I'd travel to Chicago. New challenges. New friends.

My parents shared my enthusiasm. Together, we had a commitment to Christ. We respected and loved each other. I'd miss them.

But my mind was on Chicago, and my emotions flowed toward the future. I was intent on exploring new worlds.

They sent letters several times a week. At Christmas and Easter they welcomed me as if I'd come home from East Asia. But what did they really feel?

I got a hint not long after I left them. I met Jeanette in Wisconsin and took her to Pennsylvania at Christmas. I put the ring on her finger, and we walked into the kitchen to make our announcement.

Amid all the congratulations and smiles and joy, someone sneaked in the words, "Well, Harold, you didn't get your girl from Pennsylvania, did you?" It was meant to be humorous, a side remark, filler. But it came up out of a deep yearning. A Wisconsin girl meant less chance I'd live nearby. Why did they have to think about that?

There was only one way I would ever understand. Later, Jeanette and I had a baby girl, Michelle. Then a little boy, Todd. And now, Greg.

How can I describe my emotions toward them? Holding them. Talking to them. Throwing them into the air. If anything happened to them, it would slice deep. I love them like . . . like I love Jeanette.

And I guess that's the parallel.

I used to dream of finding *the* girl. Building a life together. Enjoying each other. Planning together for a lifetime. I always knew that, once in love, breaking apart would be like sawing me in half.

And now, it's the same with Michelle and Todd and Greg. Until I was a dad myself, I never dreamed my love for them would be as strong as my love for Jeanette. Or that breaking from them would be as tough in some ways as if Jeanette were to leave me.

Oh, I don't intend to become a clinging parent. Mine weren't. But as my children grow toward all the excitement of their futures, they won't feel what I will: this oneness with them. They'll be all wrapped up in college or engagements or careers.

So, I'm psyching myself to enjoy freeing them a little at a time, then to enjoy watching them fly from the nest with their own strong wings. Sure, I'll smile and laugh and share their enthusiasm as they leave. But I don't expect them to look back and understand all my feelings. I didn't a few years ago. I had to have this bond with Michelle and Todd and Greg to understand what my parents felt the day I packed that Datsun. Their tears mixed with their hugs and handshakes meant more than a warm ritual—it was a ripping of fabric, like birth ripping through the living tissue of a new mother.

It's natural—the mixture of pain and joy. But somehow I wish I'd understood all that the day I hugged Mom and Dad goodbye.

WHEN YOU DOUBT YOUR PARENTS LOVE YOU

Philip Yancey

S tart at the maternity ward. Behind a glass case you will see row after row of shriveled, red babies, squirming feebly and crying in unison. Look closely. Their eyes are swollen shut, their heads may be temporarily flattened by the trauma of birth, their hair is thin and scattered. Not very appealing. If you saw such a product in a Sears catalog, you'd quickly flip the page.

Now go to a room where new parents are holding a wrinkled, red baby. Surprise! They are grinning and laughing and poking it and exclaiming how beautiful—yes, *beautiful*—it is. And they're serious! The woman you see has just spent the most physically demanding day of her life tearing flesh and muscle to push that baby out, and she's absolutely convinced that every second of the ordeal was worth it.

But don't stop with the maternity ward. Go on to the intensive care unit and ask to see the rooms where teenagers stay. One or two kids will be suffering from car accidents. Puffy scars crisscross their faces, and plastic tubes spill from their noses, throats, and abdomens. Perhaps a girl is there because of a fall from a horse. One is dying of cancer.

You may not be able to see the kids, but in the waiting room you will see their parents. They're always there. Come back in five, ten, or twenty hours: They will still be waiting. Nothing else in the world matters to them but that bruised hunk of tissue kept alive by plastic tubes. The father may be working two jobs, paying thousands of dollars to keep his daughter alive. The mother has dropped out of everything: She goes to no meetings, she sees no friends. Her life is the hospital. Maybe she and her kid fought often, but that doesn't matter now. She is there, waiting. She will be the first face her daughter sees if the girl regains consciousness. The mother will devote months to her daughter's recovery. She will clean her child's bed, bathe her, cheer her up, buy her presents—anything. Nothing else matters.

Hospitals show parents at their best.

But perhaps the nitty-gritty of living with kids shows them at their worst.

Your parents may seem unwise, confused, or out-of-date (just as you will seem to your kids someday). At those times, what helps most is to believe—*really believe*—that they love you. If you ever doubt that, there is one easy cure—visit a hospital.

"You want the garage key so you can get the car *out*? You're never satisfied, are you?"

THE DAY MOM CRIED

Gerald Moore

C oming home from school that dark winter's day so long
ago, I was filled with anticipation. I had a new issue of my
favorite sports magazine tucked under my arm and I'd have the
house to myself. Dad was at work, my sister was away, and
Mother wouldn't be home from her new job for an hour. I
bounded up the steps, burst into the living room, and flipped on
a light.

I was shocked into stillness by what I saw. Mother, pulled into
a tight ball with her face in her hands, sat at the far end of the
couch. She was crying. I had never seen her cry.

I approached cautiously and touched her shoulder. "Mother?"
I said. "What's happened?"

She took a long breath and managed a weak smile. "It's
nothing, really. Nothing important. Just that I'm going to lose
this new job. I can't type fast enough."

"But you've only been there three days," I said. "You'll catch
on." I was repeating a line she had spoken to me a hundred
times when I was having trouble learning or doing something
important to me.

"No," she said sadly. "There's no time for that. I can't carry my
end of the load. I'm making everyone in the office work twice as
hard."

"They're just giving you too much work," I said, hoping to find
injustice where she saw failure. She was too honest to accept
that.

"I always said I could do anything I set my mind to," she said.
"And I still think I can in most things. But I can't do this."

I felt helpless and out of place. At age sixteen I still assumed Mother could do anything. Some years before, when we had sold our ranch and moved to town, Mother had decided to open a day nursery. She had had no training, but that didn't stand in her way. She sent away for correspondence courses in child care, did the lessons, and in six months formally qualified herself for the task. It wasn't long before she had a full enrollment and a waiting list. Parents praised her, and the children proved by their reluctance to leave in the afternoon that she had won their affection. I accepted all this as a perfectly normal instance of Mother's ability.

But neither the nursery nor the motel my parents bought later would provide enough income to send my sister and me to college. I was a high school sophomore when we sold the motel. In two years I would be ready for college. In three more my sister would want to go. Time was running out and Mother was frantic for ways to save money. It was clear that Dad could do no more than he was doing already—farming eighty acres in addition to holding a full-time job.

Looking back, I sometimes wonder how much help I deserved. I wanted my parents' time and attention, but it never occurred to me that they might have needs and problems of their own.

A few months after we'd sold the motel, Mother arrived home with a used typewriter. It skipped between certain letters and the keyboard was soft. At dinner that night I pronounced the machine a piece of junk.

"It's all we can afford," Mother said. "And it's good enough to learn on." From that day on, as soon as the table was cleared and the dishes were done, Mother disappeared into her sewing room to practice. The slow tap, tap, tap sometimes lasted until midnight.

It was nearly Christmas when I heard her tell Dad one night that a good job was available at the radio station. "It would be such interesting work," she said. "But my typing isn't coming along very fast."

"If you want the job, go ask for it," Dad encouraged her.

I was not the least bit surprised or impressed when Mother got the job. She was ecstatic.

Monday, after her first day at work, I could see that the excitement was gone. Mother looked tired and drawn. I responded by ignoring her.

Tuesday, Dad made dinner and cleaned the kitchen. Mother stayed in her sewing room, practicing. "Is Mother all right?" I asked Dad.

"She's having a little trouble with her typing," he said. "She needs to practice. I think she'd appreciate it if we all helped out a bit more."

"I already do a lot," I said, immediately on guard.

"I know you do," Dad said evenly. "And you may have to do more. You might just remember that she is working primarily so you can go to college."

I honestly didn't care. In a pique I called a friend and went out to get a soda. When I came home the house was dark except for the band of light showing under Mother's door. It seemed to me that her typing had gotten even slower. I wished she would just forget the whole thing.

My shock and embarrassment at finding Mother in tears on Wednesday were a perfect index of how little I understood the pressures on her. Sitting beside her on the couch, I began very slowly to understand.

"I guess we all have to fail sometime," Mother said quietly. I could sense her pain and the tension of holding back the strong emotions that were interrupted by my arrival. Suddenly, something inside me turned. I reached out and put my arms around her.

She broke then. She put her face against my shoulder and sobbed. I held her close and didn't try to talk. I knew I was doing what I should, what I could, and that it was enough. In that moment, feeling Mother's back racked with emotion, I understood for the first time her vulnerability. She was still my mother, but she was something more: a person like me, capable of fear and hurt and failure. I could feel her pain as she must have felt mine on a thousand occasions when I had sought comfort in her arms.

Then it was over. Wiping away the tears, Mother stood and faced me. "Well, Son, I may be a slow typist, but I'm not a parasite and I won't keep a job I can't do. I'm going to ask tomorrow if I can finish out the week. Then I'll resign."

And that's what she did. Her boss apologized to her, saying that he had underestimated his workload as badly as she had overestimated her typing ability. They parted with mutual respect, he offering a week's pay and she refusing it.

A week later Mother took a job selling dry goods at half the salary the radio station had offered. "It's a job I can do," she said simply. But the evening practice sessions on the old green typewriter continued. I had a very different feeling now when I passed her door at night and heard her tapping away. I knew there was more going on in there than a woman learning to type.

When I left for college two years later, Mother had an office job with better pay and more responsibility. I believe that in some strange way she learned as much from her moment of defeat as I did, because several years later, when I had finished school and proudly accepted a job as a newspaper reporter, she had already been a reporter with our hometown paper for six months.

Mother and I never spoke again about the afternoon when she broke down. But more than once, when I failed on a first attempt and was tempted by pride or frustration to scrap something I truly wanted, I would remember her selling dresses while she learned to type. In seeing her weakness I learned not only to appreciate her strengths, I discovered some of my own.

Not long ago, I helped Mother celebrate her sixty-second birthday. I made dinner and cleaned up the kitchen afterward. Mother came in to visit while I worked. I was reminded of the day years before when she had come home with that terrible old typewriter. "By the way," I said. "Whatever happened to that monster typewriter?"

"Oh, I still have it," she said. "It's a memento, you know . . . of the day you realized your mother was human. Things are a lot easier when people know you're human."

I had never guessed that she saw what happened to me that

day. I laughed at myself. "Someday," I said, "I wish you would give me that machine."

"I will," she said, "but on one condition."

"What's that?"

"That you never have it fixed. It is nearly impossible to type on that machine and that's the way it served this family best."

I smiled at the thought. "And another thing," she said. "Never put off hugging someone when you feel like it. You may miss the chance forever."

I put my arms around her and hugged her and felt a deep gratitude for that moment, for all the moments of joy she had given me over the years. "Happy birthday!" I said.

The old green typewriter sits in my office now, unrepaired. It *is* a memento, but what it recalls for me is not quite what it recalled for Mother. When I'm having trouble with a story and think about giving up, or when I start to feel sorry for myself and think things should be easier for me, I roll a piece of paper into that cranky old machine and type, word by painful word, just the way Mother did. What I remember is not her failure, but her courage, the courage to go ahead.

It's the best memento anyone ever gave me.

A Silent Kind of Caring

Pat Vance with Philip Yancey

I was about five years old when I first realized that not everyone took off his right leg before getting into the bathtub. Because of a birth defect, my leg had been amputated when I was seven months old. There was no bone below the knee, so the foot and ankle were useless. Doctors recommended early amputation, since the leg would never develop properly.

There were times of self-pity, but I can't really say I had an abnormal childhood. My artificial leg caused some strange and even humorous events. During a kickball game in elementary school, my leg came unattached at the very moment I kicked the ball. It flew all the way to the pitcher's mound. Another time I took a step and my leg came off and clattered to the floor in the school hallway. When school began each fall, I would freak out the new kids by reaching down to adjust my socks and suddenly twisting my leg around backward.

Generally, people were kind and accepting about my condition. I could run and play sports, and as long as I wore long pants, it was difficult to tell I was an amputee. The roughest part was probably in Phys. Ed. I was stuck in a class with kids with heart murmurs, asthma, and hernias. I couldn't wear shorts, because that made my leg obvious. And there were embarrassing moments in the locker room when someone new would find my leg in the locker while I was taking a shower.

Only one thing about my leg caused great pain: the operations. Bone kept growing and pushing against the flap of skin where my stump ended, causing inflammation. Then I could hardly walk, so fifteen separate times I went into the hospital and had the bone scraped back. It put me out of commission for three months each time, and I would try to keep up with schoolwork by using private tutors.

My childhood might have been absolutely miserable, however, except for one person—my father. I was never that close to Dad. He was an engineer, not a very vocal person, and he didn't express his emotions easily. He was fifty-two when I was born, and I can imagine the grief it caused him to have a deformed son after so many childless years of marriage.

When I came home from the hospital, Dad examined the artificial limb they had fitted me with. It was a tiny wooden leg with a lacer around the thigh, and with shoulder and waist straps. Despite the harness, the leg kept detaching. My mother says she cried when she saw the contraption, all rawhide and wood and steel wrapped around a tiny baby. I would have to be fully undressed just for a diaper change. Dad was sure I would never learn to walk with a device like that.

So my dad did an amazing thing. He quit his job as a space engineer and signed up for a one-year apprenticeship with a limb maker. He drew no salary the whole year. At that time, the artificial-limb business was using crude designs and materials. Limb makers worked with drawings, rather than plaster casts which would have shown the stress points better.

Dad made a plastic duplicate of my stump and experimented with fiberglass and resin materials. He baked the socket for my stump in the kitchen oven, filling the house with a terrible odor.

But it worked! I was walking on Dad's new leg design before I was ten months old. And Dad never stopped tinkering. Each year he came out with an even more improved model. I needed a new leg often anyway, because my left leg was growing normally. His custom limbs required no straps and buckles to hold them on; they fit over my stump as easily as an old shoe fits over a foot.

Each year as I went through the physical and psychological strain of an operation, Dad absorbed the financial strain. The operations cost two to three thousand dollars apiece. He never complained or tried to make me feel bad for causing so much work. If I ever had a problem, he would stay up all night in his shop, repairing my leg so I could wear it to school the next day.

As I said, Dad and I were never especially close. Especially in my teenage years, we went through the typical hassles. I'm sure I didn't express love for him as I should have, and I'm sure I will never fully appreciate all he has sacrificed for me. Really, isn't that true of all kids and their parents?

I think that sometimes we do overemphasize the "warm, fuzzy feelings" side of love. We think there can't be love without an obvious emotional display. Many of my friends get hung up on that. Their parents don't really know how to relate to them; they seem distant and aloof, and my friends just assume their parents don't love them.

Well, I've concluded that parents show their love in many different ways. Sometimes it's through cleaning up after their kids have vomited all over the new carpet. Sometimes it's through letting kids go out with people they really don't approve of, or through paying for a college education when they really want you to go to another school.

And in my case, it's pretty obvious how Dad showed his love to me. You can see the proof in file drawers full of designs and blueprints of my legs, and a whole workshop built to manufacture them. He's in his seventies now, still working, hoping to come up with an improved version next year.

NEVER LETTING GO

George Lanning

I got my first "real" set of parents when I was fifteen. Before that I lived on the street, sleeping in parked cars, all-night laundromats, city parks, or at friends' homes. Once I lived with my baseball team's manager for three months, and another time I holed up in an empty football stadium.

I lived that way because my stepfather beat me. Not for any reason I could determine. Often, after a beating, he would tell me, "Now that's for what you're *going* to do!" Meaning, I guess, that discipline was a kind of bank account into which he had to make deposits to cover my future withdrawals. I never understood what made him tick.

When I was twelve years old he told me to get out or he'd kill me. I didn't know if he was serious or not, and since my mother didn't offer to intervene (she was too afraid to stand up against him) I thought I would take the hint and get out.

So by the time I was fifteen I had seen much of the dirty underside of life. And I had participated in some smear campaigns of my own—the dirt kind of rubs off on you.

I thought everyone lived like I did, in his own way. I thought that's what life was like. Until I met Kathy.

Kathy was the finest thing I had ever seen. She was smart and popular, with the kind of smile that would make you give up whatever might keep you from being with her. Most importantly, she liked me as much as I liked her.

She was "the girl" for me, forever. She was the first person I had ever known who cared about me; she put up with me in all my foul moods and gross behavior. And I idolized her for it. Kathy was my best friend.

Kathy was a Christian and I hadn't known her very long before I found out what the inside of a church looks like. Her family went to church every Sunday. Seeing it as an opportunity to be near her, I went too. At the youth meetings on Sunday nights, I would be the first one there in the evening and the last to go home at night (usually because I didn't have any place to go at night anyway).

One Sunday the minister spoke on John 3:16. He asked us all to put our names in the verse, and I went along with it. I ran it through my mind: "For God so loved George Lanning that he gave his only Son, that if George Lanning believed in him, he wouldn't die, but would have eternal life." Something clicked in my mind and I knew God was calling me. I answered.

Kathy thought it was wonderful. She worked to keep me on the upward climb. Whenever my feet wandered from the "true path" (they wandered down every bend in the road), she brought me back. She kept me involved with school, church, and other people. She lavished more time and love on me than a dozen social workers could have.

Our church soon acquired a new music director who took over our evening youth meetings. One night after everyone else had gone home, he and I were locking up the place. "Where are you going to sleep tonight, George?" he asked matter-of-factly. He knew my situation since it was no big secret.

"The park, I guess," I told him. I hadn't given it much thought.

"No," he said, "you can stay with my wife and me tonight."

I stayed with them that night, and the next . . . and the next two months of nights. Clean sheets, my own bathroom, a kitchen with a refrigerator—I had it made. I was beginning to wonder how long a good thing could last when they decided to make it permanent. Legally it was no hassle; I had been deserted by my real family. So I was adopted, and my family was expanded by two. I was on top of the world, for a while at least.

You might say I had character flaws, rough edges I had picked up in the streets. What I had thought was normal, acceptable behavior, I began to see was not normal or acceptable in a family relationship.

My new parents began a full-time remaking process on me; I had to be cleaned and polished for society. One by one my quirks were ironed out—but not without a lot of pain.

Lying was one of the first flaws they tackled. Somehow I had gotten the idea that it didn't matter what you said when you talked to someone. When my parents asked me a question, I would tell them anything that came to mind—sometimes to cover up something I had done, but most often just to make conversation. Lies were all I knew. They got me in constant trouble, but, too dumb to know any better, I stuck by them. I would lie even when there was no point in lying. When someone asked me what time it was I would look at my watch and tell them 5:00 when it was actually only 3:30. It was all the same to me.

But my new parents took a hard line on the matter. And it was strange to see how I reacted to it. In the past, if I had been caught lying, my stepfather would take his shoe and beat me around the room. I would cry, but inwardly I would spit in his eye and go right on lying.

It wasn't like that with my new father and mother. When they would look at me with that expression of disappointment and hurt—as if I had just violated a sacred trust, or wasted the family income—I would melt. I couldn't stand up to that kind of concern. They loved me more than I could know, and *why* they did I never could guess.

Sometimes that love hurt.

I had been in and out of school, luckily more in than out, since the sixth grade. Education never had been one of my passions, and grades were merely something to keep teachers happy. They had nothing to do with me. My parents took another view.

When I was a junior in high school I learned I was failing algebra. I was going right down the tubes and couldn't have cared less. But my father had enough concern for both of us. He insisted I apply myself, insisted I could learn it, insisted I study. When that didn't work he called my algebra teacher and both of them ganged up on me. My teacher came by the house every

"Here, I brought you my mother's recipe for meat loaf."

morning before school and picked me up. I arrived a half-hour early and spent that time in his class, working with him on algebra. When the next round of grades came, I passed. No one was more amazed or pleased than I was.

I had to be helped in other areas, too. I was barely scraping by in many other subjects, and the reason was TV. It didn't matter what was on, if the TV was operable, I would watch it. I gave it my all. Every spare minute went into TV watching.

But to show me that there was more to life than reruns, my folks severely restricted my viewing time. Often they had to be downright sneaky. They took to swiping the cord to the set whenever they left the house. I would howl, but there was nothing I could do about it. After a while I would settle down and hit the books. Slowly I was learning the right way to live.

Once in a while I would have a relapse, however. Every time I did something wrong my parents found out. It was uncanny. It wasn't as if they went around checking up on me all the time They just had this unfailing sense, an antenna that picked up trouble. (They also knew most of the people in town—that helped.)

One time my parents had gone out for the evening. I had the place to myself, and to demonstrate that fact I decided to light up a cigarette, something I knew they disapproved of. I went to the bathroom and smoked my cigarette and didn't think anything more about it until my parents came home.

"What's burning?" my mother asked, sniffing around.

"It seems to be coming from the bathroom," said my father.

"Uh—I know, let's check it out," I volunteered. And we all three trooped into the bathroom and looked at the light fixtures and the ventilation system. Of course there was nothing there. "Oh, my friend Joey was over." I started making up a story to cover my embarrassment. "He started smoking and I told him to put it out, but he wouldn't. He must've come in here to finish it."

Nothing more was said about the matter. I thought I had handled the scene rather smoothly. I went on with my life like nothing had happened.

Later that week came the church-sponsored banquet for all high school kids, a very big deal. We were all going to be dressed up, with flowers for our dates and all that. I had bought a new sport jacket with slacks to match. Kathy had bought a dress and shoes, and was looking forward to the big event with great anticipation.

The whole thing fell apart when my parents announced I couldn't go. My life passed before my eyes. What had I done to deserve such heartache and sorrow? Then it hit me: the cigarette story. I had *lied* to them about the cigarette and they had found out. Lying had done me in again. Kathy cried when I told her.

Her parents were upset with me. My parents were upset with me. The only person who wasn't upset with me was the banquet speaker who was staying at our house. Time was running out, but he convinced my parents to let me go to the banquet after all. I was elated—but then came the crusher. I could go to the banquet, but *without* Kathy. I was sick.

I called Kathy with the bad news and she took it hard but agreed to make the best of it. She had an ace up her sleeve—another guy, whom she didn't particularly care for, had asked her at the last minute. She could accept a date with him and still go to the banquet. I would go alone and at least we'd be able to see each other.

I watched her across the room and all night long the only thing I could think of was, "Why did I have to lie to my parents?" The thought nagged me, haunting the banquet. I was miserable over my stupidity, and vowed never to lie to them again. The cost was too great.

I guess that was one incident where I learned another side to love. Love isn't merely saying nice things to someone, giving that person a warm, fuzzy feeling. Love can be tough. My parents loved me enough to do what they thought was best for me. I needed a lesson in love, and I got it.

As important as that banquet was at the moment, my future was even more important. And my parents cared. Discipline to them was not a checking account, but a long-term investment: an investment in me.

EVEN THE WORST CAN GET BETTER

Understanding your parents' point of view helps, but it's not enough to make problems disappear. Family problems are more common than colds in January—and far more deadly. Are there any sure-fire cures? No. But lots of people have found treatments that helped them survive to better times.

The next few chapters let you experience a variety of families working on living together. Divorce, suicide, one-year silences, life-long separation—all tell what they have been through. Gut-level feelings ooze out, from deepest despair to high-flying elation. These people have faced troubles such as you may never know. Their lessons, however, are open for anyone to learn from.

These stories, troubled as they are, may give you hope. You can learn from them that no matter how hard life in the family becomes, things can get better. And you can learn the qualities that keep people intact through terrific pain.

MY SHATTERED AMERICAN FAMILY

Jake Currant

T he arguments escalated during Christmas vacation. At first we could hardly detect what was wrong. Mom and Dad would stare at each other over a meal, and not say much. Mom's eyes looked hurt and cloudy, and she avoided being in the same room with one of us kids alone, as if she were afraid we'd ask about something.

But by Christmas, no one was keeping any secrets. They stood in our living room, yelling at each other and arguing. Dad would wave his huge arms and shout; Mom would say things like "How can you do this to me?" and sob. If one of us kids tried to butt in, Dad would bark, "Shut up and keep out of this."

Three days after Christmas, Mom left to stay with a friend. She came back in a couple of days, but it was too late. While she was gone, Dad had decided to leave us for good. We found out there was another woman involved, and Dad made it clear to us he preferred moving out to start a new life with a new family.

It was New Year's Day when he finally left. Snow was falling outside, and every family on the block was watching football bowl games on TV. Sensing something big was about to happen, I stayed up in my room. Dad came in, laughed nervously and said, "Well, Jake old buddy, I'm leaving. This will make you grow—it'll be good for you." I didn't respond or follow him to the door, but a few seconds later the front door slammed shut and Dad was gone.

Soon I could hear my younger brother, my older sister, and my mom in their rooms, all crying uncontrollably. I wanted to go to them, but I was too hurt myself. I just slumped on the bed and stared at the wall.

I can't express now—I can barely remember—the devastating impact of the seven months following Dad's leaving. My sister would be sitting in algebra, taking a pop quiz, and it would hit. She would start crying and have to leave the room. My mom was even weaker. I'm sure that if I had freaked out during those first months, Mom would have had a nervous breakdown. She cried every day for hours. I found myself in the weird position of having to give my mom emotional strength. Suddenly there were no parents telling me what to do. I had to figure things out for myself just to help our family survive. It was like being put in the driver's seat of a car, with no instructions or training, with people expecting me to start driving.

Some of my friends would say, "Yeah, Jake, I know how it is." They didn't. No one knows, unless he's been through it himself. I tried my best to act strong in front of Mom. My only escape was to take long bike rides—sometimes fifty miles—and cry as I rode down the highway, tears blurring my vision. When I was finished crying I would stop at a gas station to wash my face, then head home.

I went through many stages. For a long time I kept hoping my father would come back so we could all live together happily again. Slowly, I began to see how far-fetched that was. *Dad didn't want us*—that was the hardest part to accept.

In the middle of this period (I now call it the "seven months of hell") I found God. I gave my life to Jesus Christ after a Presbyterian youth group meeting. I started going to Campus Life club meetings in my high school in Cedar Rapids, Iowa, and counseled with the director of the club.

I can't say that God replaced what had been torn out of our family. That will never be replaced. But he did ease my loneliness. Mom became a Christian too. Sometimes, when we had nothing to say to each other that could possibly cheer us up, we would just read the Bible. I would turn to verses like Isaiah 41:10, "Fear not, for I am with you, be not dismayed, for I am your God; I will strengthen you, I will help you, I will uphold you with my victorious right hand" (RSV). Or we'd turn to a favorite chapter in the book of Philippians, which we had nicknamed the "happy chapter."

By the end of seven months, both Mom and I had survived the strain. Some days we even smiled more than we cried. We had made it, depending on each other and on God, and it gave us closeness that in some way softened the blow of what we had lost.

I've heard Jesse Jackson, the black preacher/politician from Chicago, tell poor black people, "Nobody's gonna help us but *us*." That was true in our family. The outside people we had tried to lean on just couldn't understand what we were going through. We had only each other—and God—to rely on.

I received a better idea of what a family is supposed to be in those few months than I had ever gotten while our family was living together. I got the picture by trying to replace what was missing from my family. I first tried all my friends. I would hang around them, visit their homes, try to replace that vast sense of loneliness by letting their families rub off on me. It wouldn't work. Always my friends let me down. If we would disagree or have a minor quarrel, I would suddenly be shut out, unwelcome. I couldn't build trust in a relationship that could be cut off at any moment. I would press too hard, try to get too close to people, and they would back off.

Desperate, I tried attending every church I could think of. I found that the youth groups, especially, were cliquish. Each one had its own set of standards of what kind of person it would let inside. Because I was from a lower-class background, I was excluded from many of them. Soon I knew that I would never find a replacement for family there.

I began to see that a family was a place in which you *belonged* above all else. You could run away, be put in jail, cut off contact with your family, but you would still belong. Those people carried your name. In some strange way you were linked together with them by cords that could never be cut. And that's why I felt so hurt about my dad—I was linked with him, and yet he'd walked out on us. He had tried to cut those cords and pretend we no longer existed.

I am still learning to trust other people. After being hurt so badly by my dad, who knew everything about me and still rejected me by leaving, it's hard to open up to anyone else. Maybe God can give me the strength for that too. I've learned how important a family is by seeing my own family shattered. Our security and trust splintered overnight. We'll never restore all that was broken.

I hear kids at school run down their families, and I can't help remembering how I used to cut down my own family. Until one day when there was nothing left to cut down . . .

Victims of Divorce

The following interview resulted from conversations among five student victims of family breakups and the Campus Life *editors.*

CL: How did you feel when your parents divorced?

ANGELA: I remember one night they went into the bedroom and closed the door. I could hear them talking and I went to the door to listen. When I heard them mention divorce I hurried away; I didn't want to hear it. I got up the next morning to find my mom crying. And my dad just kissed me good-bye and left.

I had never suspected anything. I thought my parents fought like everyone else's parents. I was confused and depressed for a couple of years. I quit doing things with my friends. I'd come home after school and mope around the house.

At times I'd go to my room, pull a pillow over my head and just scream. My dad wasn't there when I didn't get along with my mom, and she wasn't any help in my relationship with him. I got to a point where I thought I was going to have a nervous breakdown or something. A couple of times I told my mom I was going to kill myself because I didn't feel like anybody loved me. Grades and that kind of stuff didn't matter anymore. What I wanted was a loving family. Everything else seemed so pointless.

BRAD: For me the divorce was a big relief. My dad is an alcoholic. I remember waking up in the middle of the night and hearing my parents screaming. My dad would be drunk and throwing things. As a little kid, I remember being very scared. And very relieved when he finally moved out.

JENNY: My parents divorced when I was a baby, so I don't remember any feelings at the time. But once I got older and started asking questions and understanding what had happened, I blamed my mom. It seemed she didn't do anything to save the marriage. I kept thinking, *If only she'd tried, maybe we'd all be together as a family today.*

ALLEN: My parents' divorce wasn't a surprise because they'd been separated for a long time. But I still had a lot of bitterness toward my father. In fact, I once punched a hole in my bedroom wall out of sheer frustration. I'd look around at my friends and see the things, the opportunities I didn't have. And I'd think, *If my dad were here, we wouldn't have these problems.* Or, *If he were around, I wouldn't have to work just to help Mom pay the bills.*

CL: How has your parents' divorce affected your attitude toward relationships and marriage?

BRAD: I never saw commitment in a relationship. I never saw two people work out a difference or a problem. So all through high school and my first year in college, as soon as I came across a problem or a disagreement in a relationship, I'd be gone. It'd be little things, nothing major. But I wouldn't stick around to work them out.

ANGELA: As far as marriage goes, I think I'm going to be really careful before I make a commitment. I certainly don't want the same thing to happen to me.

My dating relationships have been affected. I'm careful not to make myself too vulnerable. I'm afraid of getting hurt by another man like I was hurt by my dad. When I date someone, he has to really show that he cares about me because I haven't had much of that from my dad. So I need to get a lot of support from any male person I'm friends with.

ALLEN: I think this is the area where the divorce has affected me most. I had an immature view of dating for a long time. I overcompensated by being too committed when dating. I wanted to play married. I'd seen what a lack of commitment had done in my family and I wanted to keep that from happening in my relationships. Of course, that created a lot of problems for the girls I dated.

I've talked with other people whose parents have divorced and many say they shy away from commitment. What I did was just the opposite. Both reactions can cause problems.

I do think I have a more realistic view of how bad things can go in a marriage and how hard I may have to work to keep my marriage from coming apart. Kids from families with strong marriages don't always understand the potential dangers.

JENNY: My experience has made me a little afraid as I look ahead to marriage. Dating scares me a little, too. When I begin to have romantic feelings, or when a guy acts like he's getting serious, I start worrying that it won't work out.

BRAD: I worry that I won't get to know my partner well enough before we get married, and that one little thing she keeps inside could turn into a big problem.

CL: You've all tried to learn from the negative experiences of your parents. But where do you turn to find positive models for your relationships?

MICHAEL: I'm very observant of people around me. For example, I watch my boss and his relationship with his wife. Sometimes I even ask him questions about his feelings and experience.

JENNY: I've learned a lot in my youth group where we've studied dating. And I've talked with other Christians, kids and adults, about what the Bible says about marriage and relationships.

ALLEN: I look to my youth pastor and his wife as models. And some other couples in our church. More than sitting down and asking questions, I just watch to see how their marriages work.

CL: What are some of the struggles of living in a single-parent family?

ANGELA: I've been forced to be independent and to take more responsibility around the house. I've learned how to use a knife to fix the oven.

We don't have very much money, so I've had to do without a lot of stuff that my friends have. My mom can't afford to buy my clothes, so all the money I make from my part-time job goes for clothes. That means I usually don't have a lot of spending money.

I sometimes feel jealous of other people. When I hear other kids complain because their dads won't allow them a later curfew, or won't let them have a car, I'm afraid I don't have much sympathy. At least they *have* a dad who's not giving them a later curfew.

JENNY: Living in a single-parent family forced me to be very responsible at an early age. Mom had to work full time, so ever since I was in the first or second grade I had to get myself and my younger sister to the bus stop on time. And after school we went to the baby-sitter's house by ourselves.

BRAD: I remember everybody sort of taking care of themselves. And the maturity that resulted made me feel different from other kids my age. That made it lonely; there was nobody at my level.

ALLEN: There were some advantages in a single-parent family. Before I was a Christian I got away with more stuff than if I'd had two parents. Mom was just too busy and too tired to always keep a tight rein. But one of the toughest things is the wear and tear on the single parent. It makes you feel bad to see your parent always on the verge of exhaustion.

ANGELA: This might just be me because I'm an only child, but living with just my mom, it seems we've lost that feeling of being a family. It's more like living with a friend. The infrequent times we do sit down to eat dinner together, it doesn't feel like a family. The only time we have that feeling is if we get together with grandparents and other relatives at a holiday.

CL: Has your parents' divorce had any positive effects on you?

ANGELA: Independence. I know that when I

graduate from college and set out on my own, I won't run home to my parents every time I have a problem.

JENNY: Independence would be one of the pluses I'd mention, too. But I'd also have to say my family situation has strengthened my spiritual life because I've had to learn to be a witness to my stepfather, who is not a Christian.

BRAD: I've opened up more to my friends. With Dad gone and Mom working, if I wanted to talk to anyone besides my sister I was out of luck. Unless I talked to a friend.

ALLEN: My experience has given me a direction in life. I want to spend my life helping people who are going through what I went through. I want to go into some sort of family counseling. I know what it's like to hurt.

CL: What role has your faith played in your experience?

ALLEN: I've been forced to turn to my heavenly Father sometimes, because my natural father wasn't there. Of course, no one, not even God, completely replaces a natural father, but I have gotten to know God in a deeper way. And I think my relationship with God has given me an understanding of my parents and a better understanding of what's been going on inside me.

BRAD: When the divorce happened, I remember asking my mother if it was God's fault. She got real upset and said no. She sat me down and explained that God is perfect and that he wants the best for me and for our family. God gives people choices, and sometimes people make wrong choices. I was confused, but the one thing that clicked in my head is that

God is perfect and wants us to be happy. And through it all I've always had confidence in him.

ANGELA: I felt totally rejected by my dad and I wasn't sure Mom loved me. That's when I remember thinking, *But God loves me, and that's enough.* Knowing he was always with me was a big help.

ALLEN: My faith has helped in a different sense. It's enabled me to realize that my father's not the bad guy. He's still the man my mother fell in love with. The man God created. That's made it easier to forgive him. Mom's helped with the forgiveness, too. She's always taught me that I ought to love my father, even when I can't love the things he does.

CL: What have you learned about getting along with stepparents?

MICHAEL: I have found that a stepparent situation forces you to be so stinking mature. You're always walking a fine line between your parent and your stepparent, trying to decide which instructions to follow and which to ignore. And then there's the temptation to play one of them against the other to get what you want.

BRAD: You're never sure who's in charge. Sometimes both parents try to be and they contradict each other. Other times neither one of them takes responsibility. You have to be ready to stick up for your rights if a stepparent does something wrong. But at the same time, you ought to let them know when they do something great.

JENNY: It's tough. Your mom is your mom and your stepfather is just this guy who comes to live with you. It's hard to accept that. But I've learned that your attitude can make a big difference. At first I didn't get along with my stepdad. But one day the thought hit me, *He's not a Christian. You ought to be a good example to him, and instead you're being so snotty.* So I decided to change.

I started talking to him more, listening to him, even having conversations with him. And this past Valentine's Day I was getting a card for my sister and my mom when I decided to get something for him, too. I'd never done that before. I didn't know what kind of card to get. I didn't feel right giving him one that said "To Dad." So I settled for one that said "You're a Special Person," and I just wrote a little something on it. Later I found out he told my mom, "Jenny's really a thoughtful girl." I'd thought all my time and effort at being nice were going down the drain. But it's not. I've noticed a nice change in our relationship that is improving things for the whole family.

ANGELA: I think you have to look at your relationship with a stepparent more as a friendship relationship. They can't really take the place of your parents. You have to treat them like friends. The most important thing is to let them know you respect them. And don't treat them like they don't belong; they belong in your family just as much as you do.

CL: What advice would you give someone who is going through or has gone through his or her parents' divorce?

ALLEN: Don't deceive yourself into thinking it hasn't affected you. It has.

For several years I told myself I'd come through my parents' divorce unscathed. But then came the day I realized the truth. And I wept like a baby because I saw how I'd messed up a relationship with a girl as a result of the problem I mentioned earlier. And then it hit me that my parents' divorce was causing me to fail at the very thing I'd vowed to succeed at—establishing healthy relationships with girls.

Divorce affects everyone in every family that goes through it. We need to understand those effects before we get into our own marriages and repeat our parents' mistakes.

The best way I've found to understand the effects of divorce in your life is to talk about it with other people who have been through it. On our campus we've begun a discussion group of kids from divorced families. We get together periodically to talk about our feelings and our struggles. I've found it to be an incredibly valuable help and encouragement. You need to talk with someone in your situation in order to identify your feelings. And you have to identify your feelings before you can deal with them.

BRAD: My best advice is that you have to be willing to accept your parents' divorce. You can always hope that they're going to get back together, but you must accept the fact they probably won't. It's frustrating to sit back and watch, wanting to do something but knowing that you can't. It hurts. But you just have to pray that God will help you make the best of it.

JENNY: I'd say, keep an open mind. And ask questions about what's going on. I think you have the right to know why it's happening. But keep an open mind to both sides, because there are going to be many things you can never know. So try not to take sides.

And if you have to choose which parent you're going to live with, make sure the parent you don't choose knows you still love him or her. And whomever you do live with, I think you need to give him or her a lot of encouragement. Try to love and encourage both parents.

So many times I would walk in and my mom would be crying. And I'd walk over and give her a hug. She needed that. All parents do. They try to look strong and able to handle things, but I think they need as much comforting and under-standing as we do.

ANGELA: Never blame yourself. A lot of kids do. But no matter how much it affects you, you are not the cause.

MICHAEL: I'd just want to remind people that God can use anything and everything to build character in us. He's big enough to use even the things that seem to be horrible to make us more like he wants us to be.

WHEN PARENTS FIGHT

Jay Kesler

D o you know what it's like to lie in bed at night, listening to your parents fight? Have you lived with the gnawing worry that your mom and dad were going to split up? It's a terrible feeling. You are no longer able to put any trust in things you once considered secure. You can feel hopeless and lost. Nobody—not your friends, not your teachers, not your brothers or sisters—has the power to affect you like your parents.

Chances are you don't constantly worry about this. You probably feel confident your family will hold together.

But when your parents fight, the problems are all you can think about. Food is tasteless when you eat meals with a family that's feuding. Sleep is disturbed when you wake to the sound of loud voices. Peace of mind is hard to find when you're caught in the middle of a fight between two people you love.

To survive you need perspective, first and foremost. You must be able to step back from the action and watch. Let's say I go to see a production of *Hamlet*. As the play progresses, I get more and more caught up in the conflict. When I see the last scene, in which everyone gets killed, I can't stand it any longer; I leap up on the stage and try to throw myself between the actors. Or maybe I'm able to sit tight, but when I leave the theater I'm so worked up that I grab a knife and stab a few people, too. You would say I was making an inappropriate response to the play. The best way to respond to *Hamlet* is to sit and watch the play and leave the theater thinking about it.

Yet if your parents are having trouble, your first reaction is to get involved. You want to leap up onstage and throw yourself between them. But you won't help anyone because you're too minor a character. At this point some of the other major characters, such as clergymen, counselors, or relatives, need to come onstage and help your parents. You can't.

Your second reaction is to go out and start acting like your parents—to start hurting your friends. Or maybe you'll even take out some of your frustrations on yourself. But obviously that won't do any good either.

The best plan is to sit tight and stay out of things. It's rough, because you can't leave the theater, no matter how much the emotions onstage get to you. If you remember that you only have to live with this for a few more years, you may be able to grit your teeth and learn from it. The lessons will be invaluable for your future.

I'm not suggesting you do nothing, just that you know your limits. You can express your feelings and clear the air between you and your parents. Perhaps you can find a good time to sit down with them—when they're not fighting—and tell them how they're affecting you. Choose a time when it's quiet—just before bed, dinnertime, Saturday morning—and be honest with them. You might be able to help your parents realize how serious their fighting is. But you can't solve their problems for them. If you try, you may get crushed in the middle of forces you're not strong enough to master. You should carry your end as well as possible—try not to mouth off, try to understand their problems, try to be pleasant. But you're not a family counselor. You can't sit them down and say, "Come on, Dad, we've got to straighten things out." Whenever your parents look at you, they remember when you wore diapers. They can't imagine any smart advice coming out of you.

You aren't going to single-handedly straighten out your family's problems. The most important thing is to keep your own head screwed on straight. It isn't easy. You may find these days to be the most emotionally trying of your entire life. But survival is possible. Here are some general principles I'd suggest:

Never take sides. That won't be simple, because in any situation it will appear to you that one side is right and the other wrong. But when counselors dig deeply into the causes of family strife, they nearly always discover two sides to the story. Things are not as they appear.

Suppose your dad comes home from work and seems quite irritable. Your mother says something, he overreacts, and it develops into a fight. At first you might feel protective of your mother and think, "Dad has no right to jump on her that way." But there may be a number of hidden factors you don't know about. For one thing, you don't know the kind of pressure your dad has been facing all day. He may be watching younger friends get laid off, or he may be worried about losing his job at forty years old. All of that may be involved in his being irritated at home.

"Well," you say, "it's not my mom's fault." But that isn't how a married couple looks at problems. If he's under that kind of pressure your mother ought to be helping him cope. Maybe she's not holding up her end. And maybe she's coping with pressures you don't understand.

Perhaps they're having sexual problems. How are you going to know about that? There are too many possibilities for you to even think about taking sides intelligently.

Even if you could, taking sides wouldn't help. Family problems will not be corrected if you go around trying to determine who's to blame and who isn't. The blamed party will feel guilty or angry, and the blameless party will feel self-righteous. Solving a family problem requires determined action by *both* parties.

Accept your parents, weaknesses and all. You can't do that if you believe in the prevalent American myth of the well-rounded person. There simply aren't any well-rounded people. Everybody has a bad side, a weak side. Everyone has needs, and that's why working together is such an important aspect of Christianity. We all complement each other. If there were well-rounded people, they wouldn't need complementing.

So when looking at your parents, don't go looking for their faults. Look for their strengths. One person may have an excellent ability to love and accept, while another person's abilities lie in organization. Believe me, they're both essential; one isn't *better* than the other.

Be realistic. Remember that all families go through cycles. There are times when your parents are under more pressure than at other times. Don't freak out because one week is bad. Things sometimes get bad in the normal course of events, but they also get better.

Don't compare. You may think a certain girl's dad is really nice when you're there, and you may wish your own father were like that. But you see her dad only in a good light—he's not going to spout off while you're around. He's in a totally different role with you—for instance, he's not in charge of disciplining you. So naturally, he comes off a little better.

Families are different from one another. How your parents act toward each other partially depends on their backgrounds. Certain ethnic groups tend to express themselves more. Maybe you're from an Italian family, and your parents argue loudly, yet without hostile feelings. You go to high school with a lot of kids from English or Scandinavian backgrounds, and you wish like crazy for the peace and quiet you find in their homes. But keep in mind that their homes aren't necessarily better just because people express themselves differently. Maybe that calmness is covering a feud. A silent feud is worse than an argument any day.

So don't just watch the arguments; watch for the kissing, the loving, and forgiving. If your dad loses his temper and yells at your mom, but the next thing you know they're cooing and cuddling, and you're the fifth of eight kids—relax. It's just their style to yell. On the other hand, if you don't see overt signs of affection between your parents, it's not necessarily because they don't love each other. Some people come from homes where love isn't expressed by talking or touching. It's expressed by duty, like in the musical *Fiddler on the Roof:* "Whaddya mean, do I love you? I wash your socks, milk the cow, have your children. Of course I love you."

I suppose the most common reaction when your parents have problems is anxiety. You lie awake at night listening to them fight, and a cold shadow creeps over your life; everything that means warmth and security clouds over.

Fighting that helpless feeling is like fighting quicksand; you only wear yourself out as you sink deeper and deeper into it. It can make you paranoid and afraid. It can make you talk too much or clam up with your problems.

So don't fight it; learn from it. When you feel desperate and panicked, think about your parents feeling exactly the same way. They probably do. They are already straining with anxiety over growing old. Most people are very frightened of middle age and old age. They realize how economically vulnerable they are; at that age, what does happen if you lose your job? The frustrations of marriage, which they probably thought would be their dream-come-true, add to that. They are going to be living with those problems the rest of their lives, while you just have to survive two or three more years with them.

You're probably just one of a family of anxiety-ridden people. Realize that, and you'll be able to empathize with your parents. You will be able to talk to them better, understand them better. You will even find yourself feeling sorry for them, which in small doses isn't all bad.

Those feelings of anxiety can do even more for you; they may drive you to the rock bottom source of security. Only one thing absolutely cannot fail you no matter how rotten you are or how rotten the world is: God's love. Everything beyond that is a bonus. Maybe you have one friend in the world. That may seem bad, but actually that one friend is a precious bonus. You weren't guaranteed any. Maybe you're doing well in school, and you're going to get the education you need and get a good job. That's a bonus, too. Maybe you have a steady temperament, and your emotions don't soar up and down every five minutes. That's a bonus. Life is full of bonuses, and they ought to be thought of that way. The only thing that isn't a bonus, that is guaranteed, is "God loves you."

Friends can be stripped away. The security of a home can be stripped away. Warmth and food can be taken away. Your own mental stability can go out the window. The only genuinely sure thing is God. "He will keep in perfect peace all those who trust in him, whose thoughts turn often to the Lord" (Isaiah 26:3 LB). Ultimately we need to push our roots down deep enough to realize this is our only true stability.

Instead of letting anxiety about your parents drive you into a frenzy, you should allow it to drive you deeper into God's grace. Only this can really cure anxiety. Whatever love you get at home can truly become a bonus to you, an *extra* for which you're thankful.

Increasingly, problems between parents are going into court and ending in divorce. Thousands of kids must cope with their parents' separation or divorce. Maybe you're one of them. Maybe you're going to be one of them. Or maybe you just worry that you're going to be one of them.

It may help to know that it's not the end of the world. It can be very, very difficult, but even at its worst, it is the kind of thing you can live through.

Most of the principles for surviving a divorce are the same as those for surviving parental fights. You are going to want to take sides, and in some cases your parents will try to drag you into their battle. It's only natural for you to feel that one person is right and the other wrong, whether you have an accurate picture or not. This tendency grows stronger when you are living with only one parent at a time.

I would caution you, however, to maintain as much objectivity as possible, particularly by loving *both* parents. If you show a spirit of forgiveness, it'll be easier for your parents to do the same.

Often, it becomes tedious living with one parent. That parent has to be all things to you, while the other parent only comes in once in a while and treats you to nice things. Try consciously not to glamorize the parent you don't live with. Don't verbally compare the two. There are enough wounds between them without flicking off scabs.

You may feel—many do—that the divorce or separation was your fault. Even if your parents point at you, fight over you, or blame you for their troubles, it is highly unlikely that you are the cause. Psychologists and marriage counselors have observed again and again that the problems that led your parents to separate or divorce began long before you arrived on the scene, perhaps even during your parents' childhood. So whatever you do, don't blame or punish yourself for what has happened.

You are going to need somebody to talk to. Find some adult you can trust, someone who will understand, someone without any ulterior motive. Adults are usually much more open to being a friend to you than you'd think at first; in fact, most would welcome it.

Older brothers and sisters can also be a very important bridge. They may have a far deeper understanding of the problems that led to the divorce; talking to them can help. If you're an older brother or sister, I think you ought to be particularly sensitive to ways you can heal the pain in your younger brothers and sisters. Just talking things out can be tremendously healing.

Don't forget to consider professional help. Licensed counselors or therapists are trained to help you identify and work out the problems you're facing with your parents. You don't have to be on the verge of cracking up to see them. They help a lot of very normal people. Your pastor or your school counselor can probably put you in touch with someone qualified.

You know how an oyster makes a pearl? A pearl begins with some kind of irritation coming into the life of the oyster—a grain of sand, or a piece of shell. Instead of trying to expel the irritation, which an oyster can't do anyway, the oyster surrounds it with its own body fluids and gradually encases it with a smooth coating. The irritation becomes a beautiful pearl.

Extreme problems, like those with troubled parents, can have the same effect on you. If you surround them with love and understanding, gaining personal insight for your own future, you will end up with something infinitely valuable. Your life is not over. You are not doomed to failure just because your parents failed. On the contrary, you have an opportunity to grow. You can develop strength that will help you cope with all of life's problems. You can become able to help yourself and others. God can use people who know how it feels to be a child from a troubled home.

The Father Gap

Gregg Lewis

Sandra sat across the table from me and talked about her family. Sadness edged her voice as she said, "I vividly recall going home for Christmas after my first quarter of college. I was so glad to be home. I kissed my mom. And on impulse I threw my arms around my daddy's neck and gave him a giant hug. I still remember the feeling as he awkwardly reached up and gave me a sort of reluctant, one-handed pat on the back.

"That was the only time in my life I ever remember my daddy hugging me. I've never seen him kiss my mother. Not once have I ever heard him say 'I love you' to me, or to anyone else in our family. I guess you'd have to say my daddy wasn't a very demonstrative man."

Our Father, which art in heaven.

Buddy played on my Little League baseball team when I was twelve. I remember him because of his father; I can still hear the man's voice as it carried over the entire field and penetrated through the stands.

"Why'd you swing at that pitch, Buddy?"

"You gotta run faster than that if you're going to play this game."

"What a bonehead play, Buddy! You know better than that."

"Looks like we're going to have to work on that one at home until you can get it right."

"You should have gone to second that time."

"How could you miss such an easy one, Buddy?"

Game after game, week after week the man publicly badgered his son. And at the very sound of his voice you could see the muscles in Buddy's body begin to tense up. Buddy never was a very good athlete; he gave up baseball for good at the end of that summer.

Hallowed be thy name.

As early as he can remember, John's dad told John he wanted him to be a surgeon when he grew up. Once John began elementary school, his father required him to spend every afternoon and evening reading and studying. John wasn't allowed to go out and play with other kids. He never could participate in any sports; his father wouldn't sign for permission. "You've got more important things to do if you're going to make it as a surgeon." It didn't matter that John hated the sight of blood and wanted more than anything to write plays.

"I've been a high school drama and English teacher for five years now," John told me. "My students have won the top state awards in drama for the past three years. But my father feels I'm a failure because I'm not doing my residency at the Mayo Clinic."

Thy Kingdom come, thy will be done on earth as it is in heaven.

There wasn't really any bitterness in Carla's voice when she said it. But the feeling was buried there, just under the surface of her words. "I wouldn't walk across the street to meet my father if I knew where he was. In fact, I'd probably cross to the other side of the street just to avoid him—if I knew who he was. He left my mom alone with three kids when I was two. None of us has seen him since. And I for one never want to. I needed him then. But I don't need him now."

Give us this day our daily bread.
A few years ago newspapers around the country picked up a brief story of Randy, a teen-age boy who waited in an idling car while a group of his friends burglarized a small business in a Mid-western city. What gave the story a twist was that the store belonged to Randy's father.

When Randy was apprehended and his guilt proven, he asked his father's forgiveness. Instead of forgiving him, Randy's father officially announced the death of his son. An actual funeral service was held for relatives and friends. And from that day on, for his family, Randy ceased to exist.

And forgive us our debts, as we forgive our debtors.
"It was the toughest thing I ever expect to do in my life," Alice told me. "I walked to the front of the courtroom, took the oath and told the judge everything. My social worker had explained that the state would take custody of all us kids and that we might never be together as a family ever again.

"But I had to do it for my little brothers and sisters. I was sixteen; I knew I'd survive. But I didn't want the little kids to suffer any more of my father's drunken abuse.

"So I told about the beatings, the ropes, the coat hangers, the incest. Everything. In two hours of testimony I never once looked at my father. But I never forgot he was there either; I could feel his eyes on me the whole time I talked.

"That was the worst day of my life."

And lead us not into temptation, but deliver us from evil.

Recently I overheard a dorm room conversation in which an engaged guy informed his buddies: "I told Christy we had to get some things straight before the wedding. I said I didn't mind cooking every once in a while. But I was going to draw the line at washing dishes and changing diapers."

Another time I heard a father of two grade school kids brag that he'd never changed a dirty diaper in his life. And it reminded me of a sad statistic I'd read: The average American father spends less than two minutes a day with his newborn child.

For thine is the kingdom, and the power, and the glory, forever.

Perhaps you have, as I do, a human father who makes it easy to trust, love, and believe in a heavenly Father. If so, you probably ought to thank them both.

But for many people I've known and talked with, the "father" image God chose has been muddied or shattered by experiences with earthly fathers. In a lot of cases, their feelings toward a father have become an emotional chasm between them and God.

If you've suffered such a father gap, the chasm may run so deep it can't be easily bridged. However, you can ask God to help you recognize the source of your feelings when they gape in front of you. You can also ask God's help in seeing beyond the rift and working around it.

You'll probably need God's help to forgive

your earthly father. But while you still try to love your dad, you can ask God to show you other models, other people with more fatherly traits you can admire, emulate, and attribute to God.

We can do nothing to change the kind of human father we were born to. We can, however, determine that when the time comes for us to have our own children we will be the kind of fathers (or marry the kind of men) who will be so loving, encouraging, supportive, dependable, forgiving, gentle, and involved with our children that they will find it easy to believe in a God who's like their father. We need to realize this is one of marriage's worthiest goals.

God never intended us to wince every time we approach him. He wants everyone to come to him naturally, enthusiastically and warmly when we say, "Our Father, which art in heaven . . ."

Letter to an Unknown Mother

Lisa Jones

Dear Mom,

This is a letter you'll probably never receive. I have no
idea what your name is, or
where to send this. But I have
to write it. There are lots of
things I have to say and have
been wanting to say for quite
some time. This letter is the
best I can do.

It's really weird, when I
think about it. I mean, you're
my mom, but really only my
biological mother. I can't even
imagine what you look like—
and I only call you "Mom" for
lack of anything else to call
you. Do you ever wonder what
I look like? I suppose they at
least let you hold me, but I
was just a little, blond, brown-
eyed baby. My mom says I
was about the best-natured
baby she's ever seen. But I
was probably too young for
you to realize that. Sometimes

I get a little jealous of other kids. My first baby picture was taken when I was two months old, but others have pictures of when they were days or even hours old. Do you think about me much this time of the year as my birthday approaches? Do you ever wonder what I look like, what I'm doing, what my interests are? Do you ever feel guilty on my birthday?

I sincerely hope you never feel guilty about giving me up. Somehow, it was all for the best. Sure, when I was little I wanted you to hurt—I felt "deprived" for some reason. I felt I was "different" from other kids. I'd get teased a lot about not *really* belonging to my family. Yet now, I don't want you to hurt. It was hard enough for you to give me up. Maybe it'll make you feel better to know that I've had a very full and happy life. I'm musical, athletic, "funny," a dreamer and an optimist.

Now comes the big question: Whom do I take after? That one question has bothered me more than anything else. Sure, they matched me up pretty well with my folks. I look a lot like my mom and I have an adopted brother who looks so much like me that some people have thought we're twins. I have brown hair with a blond streak in it. It gets lighter and more streaked in the summer. I did have blond hair when I was little, but it got darker as I got older. I'm 5'5" tall and weigh 130 pounds. I have brown eyes, "full" lips and a nose with a bump in the middle and an overhang on the end. My hands are kind of small, my wrists are very skinny, and my feet are a *little* big.

So, after all this description, who do I look like? Do I have your eyes, Dad's nose, your hair and teeth, or what?

Sometimes, when I'm in a city or someplace new, I wonder if maybe I'm looking at you and don't realize it. Sounds weird, but it's possible, isn't it? I could even talk to you, and neither one of us would ever know. I've also wondered if I have any brothers or sisters. Do you have a family? If so, do they know about *me*?

Which brings me to yet another question. Why did you place me for adoption? I figure I'm probably illegitimate, and luckily for me, abortion wasn't practiced as much in the sixties. (I'm strongly anti-abortion.) Did you already have a family, and were you just too poor to raise one more child? Were there family troubles and you didn't think it would be a "fit" environment to raise me? Did something happen to you when I was born, and my father didn't want me? As you can see, I have a fantastic imagination. I've gone through each of these possibilities and more quite thoroughly in my mind. Did you ever want to keep me though? I can't help but think you had to, sometime.

There's one thing that I wouldn't want, though. I wouldn't ever want to meet you. Oh, sure—there was a time when that was my one passion. But now the most I'd want would be to see a picture of you, just to see what you look like. I'm telling you this because I'm pretty happy now. My family really loves me, and even though there are rough times, I still love them. And meeting you would put a strain on that relationship. I'd feel pulled in two directions, with two different loyalties. I just couldn't put myself or my family through that. Besides, I'm a closed chapter to you—a part of your past you'd just as soon forget. That's why I can never send this letter to you. It just wouldn't be fair.

I'll always have questions though. I'm going to be seventeen years old Sunday. Seventeen years of wondering. I'm probably going to wonder until the day I die. Yet I think that's only natural. It was good for me to write this letter—it's the first time I've ever been able to get out all my feelings at once. It's easier than trying to tell someone.

There's one thing I want you to know. Strange as it seems, I love you. I have no idea what you look like, why you gave me up, or if you're even alive anymore, but way down deep I *love* you. I hold no grudge against you. You see, I'm a Christian now, and as hard as it is sometimes to live like a Christian, it's so much easier to love now.

Well, that's about all I have to say. I'll probably feel this way again next year. There's something about my birthday that makes me think. But if I do, I'll just get this out and reread it—it'll do me good. I should've done this long ago!

Love,
Your daughter

LETTER TO AN UNKNOWN DAUGHTER

Anonymous

Dear Lisa,

I have read your letter four times today and decided to write you through *Campus Life*. Seventeen years ago I decided to give up my baby girl for adoption. I do not know whether you are that little girl from my past. From your description, which is very similar to mine at seventeen, you certainly could be. As I write this letter, I'll assume that you are. And I will say some of the things that I have wanted somehow to say to you for the past seventeen years.

I felt very fortunate when I had you. Yes, I did hold you and cuddle you. My social worker and my mother were both with me at the hospital and they both encouraged me to hold you if I wanted to.

And I did. I wanted to hold you because I had been talking to you for most of the nine months I carried you—talking about my life and your life and the way the world works. I loved you then, and I love you now, and I wanted to see you and hug you and tell you how much I cared about you. Did I ever kiss you! As my mother looked on, she kept smiling and crying all at the same time. She saw how much I loved you and said that she and Dad would help if I wanted to try to raise you. And they meant it.

You were a nice-looking baby. My mother took a picture of me holding you, which I would be glad to send you except . . . except that it shows what I looked like at seventeen. And now, just like then, my pregnancy is something private.

How can I explain it? I didn't want anyone to know about it then. I wanted to be free to make the best decision without my friends at school or lots of other people interfering. I worked through a lot of questions then, and have sorted through many since. And in a way that I will do my best to explain, I feel God took my mistake, my sexual sin, and made something good of it. Whatever good there was is linked to you—what you are, what you have and will become. And that one picture is important also to me—a symbol, I guess, of the good God has brought from my sin.

Honestly, Lisa, I was worried when I read about your need for a picture. For a while I thought, *Why is she wanting a baby picture when she has something much more precious? She has life. And she has parents who love her and have cared for her.* Then I thought about my own feelings and I thought about that normal curiosity we all have.

I do think about you on your birthday. It was a difficult delivery. But when I saw you, such a gift of life, it really did overshadow everything else. I had heard people explain birth that way. But until you were born, I never could have imagined it.

I have wondered about you all these years and have hoped you were doing well. Having put you in the hands of a Christian adoption agency that promised to give you a good home, I didn't really worry, but I have often wondered.

I didn't know what to make of your question, Do I feel guilty on your birthday? I thought about that for a long time. I guess you must have meant one of two things with the question. So I'll try both answers.

If you meant, do I feel guilty because of the sexual intercourse that resulted in your conception, the answer is no, not any longer. I had just turned sixteen when the boy I was dating talked me into "playing" with him in a personal way. And so, one night, partially out of my curiosity and partly because I was so naive, I lost my virginity. It happened only once. John (not his real name) promised that nothing would happen, that he knew all about sex. But his kind of contraception, withdrawal, didn't work for me. I never dated John again because of the way that evening went. I later learned that I was pregnant.

Guilty? At the time I felt enormous guilt, but as a Christian I believe that God has forgiven me. I am at peace with God and I am at peace with myself.

If you meant, do I feel guilty because I decided to place you for adoption, again the answer is no. I suppose I could have married John. My parents could have pressured his parents and we could have been married, as many have done before us and many have done since. But what would that marriage have been? Would it have lasted? The marriage between two teenagers who weren't ready for marriage and who didn't have a strong, mature love for each other would have been fragile from the start. You probably know the statistics on teenagers who marry because the girl is pregnant. Nearly all the couples end up divorced.

If we had married, you would have been "legitimate." But being legally legitimate seemed to me to be unimportant compared to being legally the child of a good Christian couple who would adopt you. To them, you would be a special gift from God. They would not mind the fact that you were born out of wedlock. You were innocent of my sin and my failure.

I would have felt guilty had I tried to raise you myself, had I brought you into my home with my younger brothers and sister. I would have felt guilty had I been faced with the conflict of trying to be your parent when actually my parents would have been raising us both. And above all I would have felt guilty had I chosen abortion. My uncle was a physician, and though it would have been legally and ethically questionable at that time, the option was open to me. I, like you, am strongly anti-abortion, but at the time I hadn't thought out all the implications.

So why did I place you for adoption? I did so, first of all, because it was the best thing for me. I wanted to finish high school and go to college. I wanted to get married and have children when I was ready for those responsibilities. And I wanted to be a successful person in my own eyes, and in the eyes of God and of society. I didn't think I could do these things if I was trying to be a parent at seventeen.

But, in the best way I knew how, I tried also to make the decision for you. I just was not ready to be a parent, and I wanted you to be proud of your parents—your *two* parents. I wanted you to have a good dad, like I had. John wasn't ready to be a father at eighteen. I knew that. And besides, could I carry you for nine months and then hand you over to him, had he been the single parent? John couldn't have handled those responsibilities. His parents would have had to raise you, and although they were good people I felt that the adoption agency would do a better job of finding parents for you.

I am glad that you're happy now. I'm also glad that you realize there will always be rough times. Times would have been even more rough had I tried to raise you.

And now I suppose there would be a strain on your relationship with your parents if we were to meet. I'm glad that you have the maturity to see this. The people who raised you really are your parents. They have a right to your loyalty and your devotion as well as a right to your flaws and shortcomings. It's part of being a family.

As I reread this letter, I am concerned. I don't want to sound unemotional and detached. I care a great deal about you, Lisa. But I have had many years to work through these questions. I have had to release you to that family that has raised you—your real family. For me to hold onto you would be a fantasy that would not be good for either of us.

In time you will need to put your fantasies about me aside, too. It is not easy for me to say that to you, but all the questions, natural as they are, must be kept in perspective.

I am glad you wrote. It is good that you expressed all those questions and feelings in a way that helps you without hurting others. You should also talk with your parents, with your pastor, and with people at the agency that found a home for you. They can be tremendously helpful in working through your questions.

There's something else about your letter. It made me write back. Like you, I've always wanted to write the letter I've just written to my unknown daughter.

In spite of my mistake, Lisa, you are one of God's special gifts. I love you!
Your biological mother

Lost to Each Other

Sue Kidd

The hospital was unusually quiet that June evening, quiet and still like the air before a storm. I stood in the nurses' station on the seventh floor and glanced at the clock. It was 9:00 P.M.

I slung a stethoscope around my neck and headed for room 712, last room on the hall. There was a new patient in 712: Mr. Williams. A man all alone. A man strangely silent about his family.

As I entered the room, Mr. Williams looked up eagerly, but dropped his eyes when he saw it was only me, his nurse. I pressed the stethoscope over his chest and listened. Strong, slow, even beating. Just what I wanted to hear. There seemed little indication he had suffered a slight heart attack a few hours earlier.

He looked up from his starched white bed. "Nurse, would you . . ." He hesitated, tears filling his eyes. Once before he had started to ask me a question, but had changed his mind.

I touched his hand, waiting.

He brushed away a tear. "Would you call my daughter? Tell her I've had a heart attack. A slight one. You see, I live alone and she is the only family I have." His respiration suddenly speeded up.

I turned his nasal oxygen up to eight liters a minute. "Of course I'll call her," I said, studying his face.

He gripped the sheets and pulled himself forward, his face tense with urgency. "Will you call her right away—as soon as you can?" He was breathing fast—too fast.

"I'll call her the very first thing," I said, patting his shoulder. "Now you get some rest."

I flipped off the light. He closed his eyes, such young blue eyes in his fifty-year-old face.

The room was dark except for a faint night-light under the sink. Oxygen gurgled in the green tubes above his bed. Reluctant to leave, I moved through the shadowy silence to the window. Below, a foggy mist curled through the hospi-

tal parking lot. Above, rain clouds quilted the night sky.

"Nurse," he called again. "Could you get me a pencil and paper?"

I dug a scrap of yellow paper and a pen from my pocket and set them on the bedside table.

"Thank you," he said.

I walked back to the nurses' station and sat in a squeaky swivel chair by the phone. Mr. Williams' daughter was listed on his chart as the next of kin. I got her number from information and dialed. Her soft voice answered.

"Janie, this is Sue Kidd, a registered nurse at the hospital. I'm calling about your father. He was admitted tonight with a slight heart attack and—"

"No!" she screamed into the phone, startling me. "He's not dying, is he?" It was more a painful plea than a question.

"His condition is stable at the moment," I said, trying hard to sound convincing.

Silence. I bit my lip.

"You must not let him die!" she said. Her voice was so utterly compelling that my hand trembled on the phone.

"He is getting the very best care."

"But you don't understand," she pleaded. "My dad and I haven't spoken in almost a year. We had a terrible argument on my twenty-first birthday, over my boyfriend. I ran out of the house. I . . . I haven't been back. All these months I've wanted to go to him for forgiveness. The last thing I said to him was, 'I hate you.'"

Her voice cracked and I heard her crying. I sat, listening, tears burning my eyes. A father and a daughter, so lost to each other. Then I thought of my own father, many miles away. It had been so long since I had said, *I love you.*

As Janie struggled to control her tears, I breathed a prayer, "Please, God, let this daughter find forgiveness."

"I'm coming. Now! I'll be there in thirty minutes," she said.

I busied myself with a stack of charts on the desk, but I couldn't concentrate. Room 712. I knew I had to get back. I hurried down the hall nearly in a run. I opened the door.

Mr. Williams lay unmoving. I reached for his pulse. There was none.

"Code 99. Room 712. Code 99. Stat." The alert was shooting through the hospital within seconds after I called the switchboard through the intercom by the bed.

Mr. Williams had had a cardiac arrest.

With lightning speed I leveled the bed and bent over his mouth, breathing air into his lungs. I positioned my hands over his chest and compressed. One, two, three. I tried to count. At fifteen I moved back to his mouth and breathed as deeply as I could. Where was help? Again I compressed and breathed. Compressed and breathed. He could not die!

"O God," I prayed. "His daughter is coming. Don't let it end this way."

The door burst open. Doctors and nurses poured into the room, pushing emergency equipment. A doctor took over the manual compression of the heart. A tube was inserted through his mouth as an airway. Nurses plunged syringes of medicine into the intravenous tubing.

I connected the heart monitor. Nothing. Not a beat. My own heart pounded. "God, don't let it end like this. Not in bitterness and hatred. His daughter is coming. Let her find peace."

"Stand back," cried a doctor. I handed him the paddles for the electrical shock to the heart. He placed them on Mr. Williams' chest. Over and over we tried. But nothing. No response. Mr. Williams was dead.

A nurse then unplugged the oxygen, and the gurgling stopped. One by one they left, grim and silent.

How could this happen? How? I stood by his bed, stunned. Wind rattled the window, pelting the panes with rain. How could I face his daughter?

When I left the room, I saw her against the wall by a water fountain. A doctor, who had been inside 712 only moments before, stood at her side, talking to her, gripping her elbow. Then he moved on, leaving her slumped against the wall. Such pathetic hurt reflected from her face. Such wounded eyes. She knew.

I took her hand and led her into the nurses' lounge. We sat on little green stools, neither of us saying a word. She kept staring straight ahead at a pharmaceutical calendar, glass-faced, almost breakable-looking.

"Janie, I'm so, so sorry," I said. It was pitifully inadequate.

"I never hated him, you know. I loved him," she said. *God, please help her*, I thought.

Suddenly she whirled toward me. "I want to see him."

My first thought was, *Why put yourself through more pain? Seeing him will only make it worse*. But I got up and wrapped my arm around her. We walked slowly down the corridor to 712. Outside the door I squeezed her hand, wishing she would change her mind about going inside. She pushed open the door.

We moved to the bed, huddled together, taking small steps in unison. Janie leaned over the bed and buried her face in the sheets.

I tried not to look at her, at this sad, sad good-bye. I backed against the bedside table. My hand fell upon a scrap of yellow paper. I picked it up and read.

My dearest Janie, I forgive you. I pray you will also

forgive me. I know that you love me. I love you, too. Daddy

The note shook in my hands as I thrust it toward Janie. She read it once. Then twice. Her tormented face grew radiant. Peace began to glisten in her eyes.

"Thank you, God," I whispered, looking up at the window. There were a few crystal stars blinking through the blackness.

Life is so fragile. *But thank you, God, that relationships, though fragile, can be mended together again . . . but there is not a moment to spare.*

I left the room and hurried to the phone. I would call my father. I would say, *I love you.*

A CHANCE TO CHANGE
Terry Hadley with Gregg Lewis

The first thing I remember was the alarm. I quickly reached over, hit the button, then fell back into bed to allow my body the luxury of two more minutes' rest. After all, it was Christmas Eve. Yet I knew I couldn't lie there long and still make it to my job at the kennel by seven. Dogs have to be fed and their cages cleaned even during the holidays.

A few minutes later I rolled out of bed, pulled on my robe, and headed to the bathroom for a shower. I was still half asleep as I wandered down the hall. So for a split second after I pushed open the bathroom door, the scene didn't register.

Then the horror hit.

My father lay sprawled on the floor in a pool of blood. My first thought was, *He fell in the shower.* Then I realized he had his clothes on. The next second I was rolling him over and crying, "Dad, Dad." But there was no response.

I reached for his arm to check his pulse. That's when I saw his wrists. Blood still oozed from the arteries there and at the elbows, which had been slashed. Two more red trails marked deep cuts across his chest.

Remembering a first-aid technique I'd seen the week before on a TV movie, I grabbed two towels and tied tourniquets around my dad's arms. Then I leaned him against the wall and propped his arms above his head.

That done, I reached for the hall phone just outside the bathroom and called an ambulance. Then I was back at my dad's side, trying once more for a pulse. I felt again at the wrists and at the neck. Nothing. His skin had already taken on a bluish hue.

When I heard the sirens screaming in the distance, I finally ran and woke Mom. The second she looked in the bathroom and gasped, she ordered me to wake my younger sister and take her next door to my aunt's.

As the paramedics arrived, I rushed my sister out the door, explaining that Dad had fallen in the shower. I didn't think she could handle the truth.

I did explain the situation sketchily to my aunt before I raced back across the yard to our front door in time to see the paramedics carry my dad out to the street. They slid him into the back of the ambulance; my mom climbed in beside the stretcher. "I'll call," she said as doors slammed shut. I stood cemented to the sidewalk, watching the flashing lights until they turned at the end of our street and raced out of sight.

Finally, I turned and walked dazedly back into the house. I felt like I'd just walked through a movie or a bad nightmare. Yet I knew it was real. My dad had committed suicide. Or at least he had tried. I was sure he was dead.

Unconsciously I found my way back to my room, shut the door, instinctively flicked on the portable TV and dropped onto the bed. I wanted desperately to be alone to sort through my numbed feelings. But my mind was a blur with an occasional flashback of the scenes—Dad on the floor, the paramedics with the stretcher, the ambulance. There were too many questions. And no explanations.

Suddenly I remembered something from the night before. Our whole family had been out Christmas caroling with a group of neighbors. As we'd gone from street to street, Dad had walked beside me. He'd said something about bills and not knowing how he was going to pay them all. I hadn't really been listening. And my only response to his concern had been a few half-hearted words like, "That's too bad," and "It'll be okay."

Now that I thought about it, Dad had seemed moody and discouraged a lot lately. I recalled several other times he had mentioned money and bills.

Maybe money *was* the problem. It could be that our family's finances were in shambles. But was that bad enough to bring on suicide? Maybe if I'd listened to Dad when he tried to talk about his troubles I could have encouraged him.

An hour of guilt and numbness passed before the phone rang. Dad was alive. His condition was critical but stable. Yet even that news couldn't penetrate the cloud of confusion, guilt, and questions in my mind. I kept thinking, "What if I'd cared enough to listen? Maybe none of this would have happened."

My two cousins interrupted my privacy a few minutes later. They suggested something I hadn't even thought of—praying. So there in my room we said a brief prayer for my dad and his recovery.

I still wanted to be alone with my thoughts. But when one cousin said, "Let's go over to our house and shoot some hoops," I agreed. Throughout three games of "horse," my well-meaning cousins kept up a constant banter about anything and everything they could think of as they tried to keep my mind off my dad. But it didn't work. I knew they were trying to be kind, but their talk did nothing but annoy me.

When we quit playing basketball, they told me they had to go downtown for some last-minute Christmas shopping. They insisted I go along. But shopping didn't ease my mind either. The canned Christmas carols coming from the department store loudspeakers reminded me of caroling the night before. The sporting goods department made me think of Dad. Everything I saw sent my mind spinning right back to him.

The next day was even worse. We went through the motions of Christmas for my sister's sake. We even went to my aunt's for a big family get-together. But the facade we put up seemed pointless; the traditions felt hollow.

Late Christmas night I sat with my mom, aunt and uncle, and grandparents and listened as they tried to analyze what had happened to Dad and why. But they didn't understand any more than I did. And their words sounded so cold that I finally got up and stormed out of the room. On the way I slammed my fist against the door and punched a hole right through it—I was so upset I felt no pain.

Over the next few days I wavered between guilty depression

over my own insensitivity, and anger at myself and everyone else who should have understood and helped Dad. To make matters worse, I avoided going to the hospital to see him. And that added more guilt to my load. But I just couldn't face him. I didn't know what I would say. What does a guy say to his own father who tried to commit suicide?

Over a week passed before I psyched myself up for a hospital visit. I still didn't know what I would say. The thought of trying to explain why I hadn't come earlier made me feel even lower. But I knew I had to go. Deep down, I wanted to see my dad.

"He'll be glad to see you, Terry," Mom said as she led me down the hall of the VA hospital. We stopped at the barred doors of the locked ward. A hospital attendant checked our IDs and let us in.

The instant I stepped into the visitors' lounge of the psychiatric wing, I spotted my dad. Sitting in a chair in the corner of the bleak, white room, wearing hospital pajamas, he looked so different. He wore a look of utter defeat, a beatenness I'd never seen in him before. The life was gone; only the shell remained.

When he looked up and our eyes met, time seemed to stand still. I waited, but the imagined questions and accusations never came. He just stared. I forced myself to smile. And then I walked quickly across the lobby and greeted him with a hug.

I still didn't know what to say; Dad did most of the talking. For a few minutes we sat and he told me about the hospital and about his daily schedule. Then he wanted to show me around.

As he directed me through the ward, I tried not to stare at people. One man, who dressed like a woman, reminded me of Klinger on the TV show "M*A*S*H." Another patient crawled around the hall barking like an angry German shepherd. "That's Nelson," Dad said matter-of-factly as we passed. "He thinks he's a dog."

I glanced sideways at my father. How could he exist with these insane people? They scared me. Yet Dad was talking in normal tones—like he belonged here. That scared me even more.

In one way, the visit wasn't as hard as I'd imagined it would be; Dad kept the conversation going. But the whole situation felt weird to me. It was as if our roles had been reversed. Dad was like a little kid wanting to show a parent around his school. And I had to be the adult who patiently followed him around and listened to him talk.

When it finally came time to leave, I gave Dad a big bear hug, and he hugged me back. The words came to me. I knew what I could and had to say. As we embraced, for the first time I could ever remember I said, "I love you, Dad."

He smiled. I promised to come back the next week. The doors opened, then clanged shut behind me. I was free. But I had a whole new set of scenes to haunt my thoughts.

Some of my guilt faded because I felt like I'd finally done something—I'd tried to show Dad that I loved him. But when I was alone with my thoughts, lying awake in bed at night, I couldn't help wondering, *What if I had cared earlier? Maybe none of this would've happened. What if . . . ?*

I realized Dad needed all the love and affirmation I could give him. But that didn't come easily; we'd never been a very affectionate family. Mom needed me, too. She began leaning on me more and more for emotional support and for help with decisions and responsibilities around the house. I felt like the whole world was sitting squarely on my fifteen-year-old shoulders, crushing me. And I wasn't sure I could take the pressure.

When a friend asked me to go on a special Campus Life club weekend called Living End, I agreed. I saw the trip as a chance to escape, to at least get away from the pressures of home for a couple of days.

I did enjoy the outing in the mountains. But even there I couldn't forget my father. In fact, on the final night, the speaker hit me right between the eyes with a talk about problems and pressures and how we can never handle them by ourselves. He explained how God could help us, no matter what our troubles are—that we don't have to struggle on our own. As the meeting dismissed he said that anyone interested in talking about the message could meet in the lodge.

Afterward, I took the shortest trail to the lodge, cornered a counselor and dumped my whole load of troubles on him. He just listened as I told him about my dad's suicide attempt, about my visit to the hospital, my concern for my mother and my sister, and the other pressures of school, work, and all the rest.

I'd grown up in a church; I'd been a Christian since I was a little kid. But I'd never really trusted God with the everyday details of life. I'd always tackled my problems by myself. And I was sinking deeper and deeper under the load. But as I talked, I realized I could let God share the burden of my problems. So right there in the lodge I prayed that God would do that. I prayed that he would take control of my life and help me show Dad the kind of love he needed.

Things didn't get instantly better when I returned home. I was still so concerned about Dad that I couldn't concentrate on my studies or on basketball practice. The coach kicked me off the team the following week.

But the next time I went to see my dad, it was easier. As I began to pray daily for Dad and for our relationship, the flood of guilt began to recede. I felt more love, more compassion toward him. The next week was even easier. And the next and the next. Gradually we began to build a kind of relationship we had never had. When he was allowed out of the locked ward we started spending my visiting time walking the grounds, swimming in the pool, shooting some baskets. And every week when I left I would give him a big hug and let him know I loved him.

After six months, when Dad finally came home again, I was still a little scared. *What if he tries suicide again?* But he didn't. He was changing. I detected a new enjoyment of life in him. I got him involved in my woodworking hobby and he loved it. A short time later he went back to work, now a different man.

However, my dad wasn't the only person who changed. Our whole family is different today, more loving and supporting of each other. I'm different, too.

My love for my family and my faith in God have grown as God has helped me accept and work out my responsibilities. The change has been gradual, but I know my parents recognize it. One day not long ago Dad came into my room, put his arm around me to give me a hug, and told me he really respects me for my faith and my life.

Finding my dad dying on the bathroom floor was a life-shattering blow for me. But God helped our family grow stronger because of it. Dad's suicide attempt was a scream for attention; we were forced to face problems we had been avoiding. Through our ordeal we have all learned how much we mean to each other, and I have come to realize how much my parents need my love and support. I'm just glad I learned the lesson before it was too late.

A Dream of What Could Be

Jon-Marc Stephens

A vision is wedged in my mind. I am almost overcome with the expansiveness of it . . . an endless blue-green sea blends into an endless sunny sky. In that vision, I am shuffling through the sand talking and laughing with my dad. The exhilarating salt air washes over my senses and my tensions are carried off with the receding tide.

That vision is a mental emblem of a relationship—my image of a friendship, a trust. But the vision is not real; it is an illusion I have created.

Instead, I walk alone down the breakwater in stormy weather. I have to get away. I have to think things through. I look up into swirling gray clouds and down into surging gray surf. The swell rises and crashes against the rocks. I am drenched to the skin. Yet somehow the dampness and cold do not bother me. It is as if this angry weather is merely an extension of my feelings, the part of me boiling inside. I wonder, are these emotions unique to me?

I recall a friend who once tried to explain her home problems to me. "Since grade school my parents have cut me down continually," she said.

I just listened.

"They don't trust me. They go through my things. They won't let me get my driver's license. They limit my social life."

I listened. But I wanted to tell her my feelings, share my fears. She was too preoccupied to listen. It seems that people are always too preoccupied to listen. Maybe that's why I enjoy this solitary walk on the breakwater; it gives vent to my unshared feelings.

I think of a week-long camping trip in the High Sierras—a family vacation. For a week our dark blue panel truck bounced over narrow, rutted logging trails as pine trees arched above us from both sides of the road. Occasionally, a family of deer would leap from the thicket, dart across our path, and disappear into the dense forest.

One night we pulled the truck into a clearing, built a fire, and roasted hot dogs and marshmallows. I watched the fire as it crackled, sending sparks swirling into the darkness. I never felt closer to my family than that night.

When did our family relationship break down? How did it happen? And why are we now so distant from one another?

A weird contrast strikes me. I think of one spring night last year. It was 9:30 and still my dad was not home. Not that it was uncommon for him to be gone. I rarely saw him. And when he was home, he and my mom fought constantly. It was that fighting that I found so intolerable—the irrational arguing and violent outbursts that followed. Having thought about the family hassles that evening, my emotions were raw even before my dad got home.

When I heard his truck rattle to a stop, I went out to meet him. Then I noticed the damage. The right side of the truck was demolished. He had been hit by a two-and-a-half-ton grain truck, he explained.

I had such mixed feelings. Was I more angry that our panel truck had been smashed or more scared of what could have happened to my dad?

My dad went inside and I walked over to the truck to inspect the damage. Within a few minutes I could hear my parents fighting. It was odd. My dad had been in a potentially serious accident. But what happened when he finally returned home? Rather than express concern for him, I was uptight over the damage to the truck, and he was already fighting with Mom.

I was furious. They argued over the most ignorant and insignificant things. And their anger sparked mine. Why do I feel more adult than my parents, more capable of a kind relationship? And what sort of glue holds together a family which seems so fragmented?

I pause and look westward, far out into the stormy sea. I taste the salt spray and consider. There is a common struggle beyond the hassles that are unique to my family.

Almost every family has its own share of turmoil—some less severe, some more severe than mine, but turmoil nonetheless. Why do families experience this push and pull for control? Why the suspi-cion? Why the contest of wills?

It is rarely absence of love, of that I am sure. Love may be poorly expressed, but through all my family's struggles, I did not doubt love.

I remember a look, one short glance, that would have assured me of love had I doubted it. My dad had picked me up late one night after work. As we drove the five miles home, he suddenly turned to me and offered an awkward apology for the family hassles. They had alienated me, he acknowledged. It was vaguely worded, but I knew what he meant. And there was just something in that brief glance in the glow of the dashboard lights. I did not doubt love.

So I wonder, why the conflicts? The outbursts of unbridled anger? And how much of the turmoil is normal, almost necessary? A natural part of the family scuffle as kids strive to gain independence while their parents strain to preserve dependence? It's hard for parents to let go; they want to feel needed (especially if their needs are not being met in their marriage). So they hang on to the kids. Like ice tongs, they hang on.

When I was younger, my dad gave me an electric train set with a circular track. The time came when he trusted me to run it alone.

One morning I assembled the sections of track wrong. The gray metal tracks snaked across the living room floor. I put the engine on the track and started it. But it kept running off the end; I had to stop it, back it up, stop it, start it, stop it. There was no continuous movement. I was always starting over.

I look at my family and realize I have inherited some misassembled track. I see that tangled track and am tempted to junk the whole train set rather than just rearrange the tracks. But if I indiscriminately reject everything my parents stand for, isn't it possible I'll toss out a lot of good with the bad?

If the track I was handed is bent or assembled wrong, I must correct it. That's part of what it means to be independent. I don't have to leave it that way. I don't have to make the same mistakes my parents made.

As the breakwater joins the beach, there is a section where the rock and sand are intermingled. I sit there on a rock and push at the sand with my feet. After that long walk on the breakwater my emotions have calmed. I study the surf and compare: after it curls and splashes, it leaves behind an expanse of harmless foam. The power is gone.

Somehow, my turmoil also will subside—the power will be taken out of it. I will sort my feelings, and, with God's help, I will reshape my values. I will not toss out everything my family stands for. I will keep what's right and put aside my bitterness over what's wrong.

And then, with my resentment forgotten, I will be free to establish a new relationship. The illusion will become reality. My dad and I will shuffle through the sand, talking and laughing as friends.

THE WAY IT'S MEANT TO BE

If your family is struggling with problems, you may tend to forget what God had in mind when he decided to group us together in families. From down in a deep rut, you can only see the walls around you. You forget there's a big beautiful world up above.

This section is designed to show you the sunshine above the rut. Its stories tell of imperfect, struggling families who have realized they have something worth struggling for. Their ideals, and their determination to learn to live up to them, represent the way families were meant to be.

A Bond Formed in Death

Interview by Amy Marshall

*Pam Cole and her mother, Wynne, have grown
to be very close. But they did not grow the easy
way. Pam sets the stage by explaining the first
major trauma they faced together.*

Pam: Dad died in his sleep in the middle of the
night. It was on a Sunday. Mom, Dad, and I had
all gone to church earlier that evening. Everything seemed so normal.

Mom woke up when she heard him groan-
ing and tossing. Then, all of a sudden, he was
quiet. The doctors termed it a cardiac arrest.

I remember coming home from the hospital
in the early morning darkness. Two very close
friends of my parents, a man and his wife, were
driving us home. Mom and I were in the back
seat.

It was so quiet, no one talking, no one
crying. I couldn't stand it. I had to say something to make everyone feel better. So I leaned
over and said, "Everything's going to be all
right." It was a statement, not a question.

"Of course everything is going to be all
right," Mom replied. She spoke with such

confidence and strength that I sank back in my seat, surprised—and also relieved.

But I had a lot of fear and some anger inside me. Dad was gone; how were we going to manage our big house without him? How could Mom afford to keep me in a private school?

My fears centered on home and school. Dad wouldn't be in the stands cheering me on during my basketball and volleyball games. He wouldn't be telling his usual jokes at the dinner table every night. He just wouldn't be there to do all the things a father does.

I didn't want to go to the funeral. I didn't want to face all the people I knew would be there.

Mom was resting on the sofa in the living room before it was time to go to the church.

"Mom, I don't want to go."

"Of course you're going. You know you'll be sorry for the rest of your life if you don't go."

"I'm not going."

I went.

The place was packed—standing room only. My whole 7th grade class was there. Coaches from the local college served as pallbearers because Dad was a Booster Club member. There wasn't a more dedicated fan anywhere than Dad.

Our whole family sat in the second row of one section. We filled the pew. My brother Brad sat on one side of me. And George, my oldest brother, sat on my other side.

I wanted to be so strong. I had always been proud of how tough I was, the girl who didn't cry, the girl who single-handedly killed spiders.

Well, I made it about halfway through, until the congregation began singing "I Am the

Resurrection and the Life," Dad's favorite hymn. I don't think I was so much sad as I was simply touched. The funeral was a celebration of Dad's going to heaven. And I know of at least one person who decided to become a Christian because of the funeral.

Afterward, my whole family, except for Mom, worried about me because I didn't show signs of grieving. I attended our basketball game the day of the funeral. I didn't play but I was there. I went back to school within a week. I just didn't want my friends at school to know my feelings.

But every other night, I'd lie in bed and cry. I thought about a lot of things then, lying in bed, that I wouldn't let myself think of during the day. It's so easy when you're busy with school and other activities to block it out. But at night, when you get by yourself, the emotions rise to the surface.

I felt so helpless. I couldn't change it. I couldn't even say good-bye.

I tried to focus on the good things. I'd think of how Dad might have been an invalid if he had lived and how he would have gone crazy because he was so hyper, just like me. Now Dad was happy in heaven. But it didn't help much. I wanted him here.

And I'd get mad at God. "What do you think you're doing?" I'd ask. "I want to know why!"

I was thirteen then, not old enough to see beyond my own hurts. Besides, Mom made it seem like she was so strong. She didn't need me.

Wynne: From the first, even on that night during and after George's heart attack, I felt God's presence. I was conscious of his tender love and care. It was almost as though I were a bystander, observing as one of his children made his entrance into heaven.

I guess I didn't worry about Pam because I know that people grieve differently. I was aware of the protective coat she was wrapping around herself, but I didn't see any harm in it.

> **Pam:** Right after Dad died, Mom and I dealt with our grief separately. We both stayed very busy, to keep from moping around too much. I eventually felt sure enough to try to comfort Mom when I could see she was hurting. I'd hear her cry and I'd go to her. Even then we didn't discuss our grief; we discussed Dad. He was and still is part of our relationship.

Wynne: We spent a lot of time talking. Both of us needed that. We missed George so much and it meant a lot to be able to talk about him.

George's death naturally pulled us together. Something as tragic as that draws you up short, and our relationship became more intense. We talked on a deeper level. I think it wasn't until George's death that Pam and I began to really pray together. We also read the Bible together, searching for answers and comfort.

> **Pam:** Mom was always reciting verses and praying about everything. She has this one special verse: "A father to the fatherless, a defender of widows, is God in his holy dwelling" (Psalm 68:5). I must have heard it a thousand times.

Wynne: I have experienced the reality of that promise. I knew from the very start that I couldn't raise Pam on my own. And there have been times when I have claimed that verse and then stood by and watched God as he has been a father to Pam.

> **Pam:** Even so, I missed not having a dad like

all my girlfriends. I didn't let it show. I didn't want any of them to feel like they couldn't talk about their fathers around me. But it was always a potential point of tension or awkwardness, sometimes even with Mom.

One night we were visiting friends. Amy is one of my best friends. Her dad, Jim, became kind of a role model to me after Dad died. This particular night, Amy and I were in some kind of a crazy mood. We were acting pretty silly, and I guess I was hanging onto Jim's arm.

On the way home that night, Mom said, "Pam, you shouldn't hang onto Jim so much."

Well, that blew me out of the water. It was like saying, "He already has one daughter. I don't think he wants to be burdened with another one."

I came back pretty strong. "Mom, I don't have a father; you could at least let me have a friend."

Wynne: I was sensitive to her need for a father figure. But that night I did think Pam was overdoing it. I knew I couldn't be both mother and father, and that was frustrating. Since George's death several men in our church have taken it upon themselves to be friends to Pam. But in the beginning we both had a lot of adjusting to do.

Pam: One of our biggest adjustments concerned the house. Mom thought we should try to sell; I couldn't stand the thought of not living in our house—the house I'd lived in since I was little. It was my home and I loved it.

Wynne: It's such a big house, much more than we really needed. I felt I had to try to sell it because I just couldn't assume we'd be able to stay. I don't think I realized how important it was for Pam to stay in the house.

Pam: I hated seeing the "for sale" sign in our front yard every time I came home. One day, after about nine months of trying to sell, I was complaining about it to Mom. She gave me this look and I shut up. Then she smiled and nodded. That was it. I raced out the front door, yanked that sign out of the ground, and threw it in the garbage.

During and after the decision about the house I could sense a new tenseness in Mom. I knew she felt a growing responsibility about financial matters. Her concern prompted me to take an interest in and be more sensitive about our finances. I've become convinced that kids should have an understanding of family finances. It helps you see things from a parent's perspective.

Wynne: Not that Pam and I always came to see eye to eye on everything. We had our share of the typical mother/daughter squabbles about cleaning her room, getting to bed at a decent hour, and things like that.

Grades were a tension point the first two years of high school. She didn't make them a priority because she was involved in so many other things. I'd get on her a lot about studying and she'd just say, "Don't bug me about it, Mom." But I knew she could do a lot better. Eventually she did; the last couple of years she's made the honor roll.

Pam: Sure, we'd fight. Sometimes we'd disagree about whether or not we could afford something. Then there were arguments about grades and bedtime. Mom has had a hard time accepting the idea that I don't need as much sleep as most people.

There were lots of other little things. I wouldn't like a new rule or the fact that I couldn't do something I really wanted to do, and I'd go storming up to my room, slamming the door.

I'd lie on my bed, wondering if Mom would come up. But she wouldn't. Now I know she was downstairs, praying that God would take over.

Wynne: There were times I simply had to pray and ask God to be the father to the fatherless. Sometimes I'd realize my rules or requests had been unreasonable and I'd back down. Always within twenty-four hours of a quarrel we'd be reconciled. We'd either agree on which of us had been wrong, or Pam would at least agree to go along with my decision.

Pam: I remember a time when I got sick and tired of her always telling me what she expected me to do. I had gotten so caught up in things at school and church that I really was neglecting my duties at home. When I realized what I'd been doing and not doing, I decided to put an end to Mom's nagging by doing it all—before she could tell me to. I realized I'd been wrong, so I prioritized some of the different areas of my life so I could do what I needed to do for Mom. And now she doesn't have anything to nag me about.

Except for my room.

Wynne: Sometimes I forget Pam is only a high school senior. She has come a long way from that thirteen-year-old, self-centered kid. We've become very close. Much closer, I think, than would have been possible if George were alive. A husband and wife relationship requires so much time and energy. With it being just Pam and me, our relationship has deepened. Not only did George's death bring us closer, but there is naturally more time for us to spend together.

I see so many parents who don't have a

strong relationship with their children and it saddens me. Praying together and trying to learn from the Bible are two things that have helped us strengthen our relationship. And of course, communication is crucial. We talk about everything. I try to focus on things that interest and concern her, but it goes both ways. She wants to know everything that's going on with me, whether it's a financial decision I have to make or something personal. And I find myself confiding in Pam. Some nights we'll sit at the dinner table long after we've finished eating, just to get caught up with each other.

Pam: Our relationship is in a transitional stage right now. I'm getting ready to go to college, yet I'm still here, living under Mom's authority. In some ways I don't want to be dependent anymore, but my mom is my friend and my main Christian role model. I cherish the open and honest relationship we have. I realize many people don't have that with their parents. But it's certainly worth working for.

Wynne: Once, when Pam was fifteen, she sent me this "Thank-you" card for Mother's Day. I pull it out and read it every now and then because it picks me up and reminds me what our relationship means to me. It says, "Mom, you're so special! I really can't thank you enough for who you are and what you are to me. The Lord has blessed me with an understanding, wonderful, beautiful mother. I'm so glad I can talk to you not only as a daughter, but as a friend also. It's so neat to be able to share my experiences with you. You're the most special person to me in the world!! I love you!"

Pam: Maybe our relationship is so strong because we've been through so much together. One day about three years ago, Mom and I were outside. I was across the street and called for her to join me. I saw her start to run. Then she just stopped. She couldn't run. Suddenly her left leg was just too weak to do it. She called the doctor and we started a round of tests. Nothing showed up positive. Doctors disagree on the diagnosis. She's been very brave; she never complains. But it's been awfully hard on her the past few years.

It hurts me to watch her on her "bad days." I sometimes feel guilty about not doing more around the house. We've both had to adjust. And I guess I do enough; we get by.

I remember one day, Mom and I were sitting in the living room and I ran my finger along the top of the end table, noticing how dusty it was.

Mom said, "Well, I guess we really should dust."

"I guess so," I said. But neither one of us moved. Then we started laughing. Why dust for just the two of us? It would have been different had we been expecting company.

Wynne: The adjustments haven't been easy. I know when Pam found out about my illness, she cried. But even when I was in the hospital, she was my tower of strength.

And now, on the days I feel discouraged about my physical weakness, Pam comes through with reminders about how trustworthy God has been and how she knows I'll be okay. She'll even remind me about claiming God's promise to be the husband to the widow and the father to the fatherless.

She's sensitive to my feelings and can always tell when I'm discouraged or feeling weak. And I don't try to hide it. We try to be open with each other about how we feel.

I could be fearful about my mysterious disease, but I'm not going to be. In John 14:1, Jesus said, "Do not let your hearts be troubled. Trust in God; trust also in me."

Pam: There she goes again, reciting Scripture. Sometimes when I see her suffering, I get mad at God. Why doesn't he just heal her?

She's already been through so much. My dad was her second husband to die. And now this. It seems like there's one thing right after another. I just want things to be normal.

Wynne: But the pain, both physical and emotional, and even the financial strain, are teaching us to rely on God.

Pam: I know Mom's right. And I know God is using all of this to help build my character. Through Dad's death, and now Mom's illness, I've learned I can't rely on my parents' relationship with God. I have to have my own relationship with him. And I really think it's taken everything I've gone through for me to reach that point.

Wynne: Pam has developed her own spiritual strength. Sometimes when I'm down about my illness she will say, "Mother, you're not going to give up." And I don't. She has a positive spirit. I know she prays for me. And I realize: I need her strength, too.

We strengthen each other by watching, doing, and sharing. And if there's one thing I'd like to say to other families, both parents and kids, it's this: One of the most important things family members can do is to affirm each other.

Pam constantly affirms me—how I look, how I've been a good example, how much she appreciates some little thing, etc. I'm afraid I've been late in learning the significance of this in the life of a family. But finally, through all that's happened to us, I'm beginning to understand the importance of telling others how terrific they are.

We need to take advantage of every day, to say "I love you" or "I appreciate you" and try to get beyond the reluctance or embarrassment we feel in expressing those feelings. When we don't say those things we withhold from each other something we all sorely need.

A son or a daughter can be a wonderful source of comfort and support to the grieving parent, the suffering parent, the discouraged or tired parent. Children, perhaps more than other people in the world, have the potential of pouring the oil of healing over their parents' hurts. I know I've experienced it through Pam and my older children—who've been incredibly supportive. And that's what family love is all about.

The Reasons for Families

Tim Stafford

Why did God choose to use families to raise us? Why not have us born fully mature, or at least able to fend for ourselves as many animals are? God could have designed the world any way he chose; wouldn't it be possible for him to work around the long, agonizing power struggle that often is part of growing up in a family?

So many families are bad, wouldn't it be better to do without?

I do not know all the reasons God chose to use families. But I can think of a few. The first is hinted at when Jesus begins to pray by calling God "Our Father." God is not, strictly speaking, our father; but we need a model to help us understand what our relationship to him is. It is found in the family. (In a few places, the Bible describes God's love for us as a motherly quality, too.)

So one reason God raises

us in families is to inform us of what he is really like. Thanks in part to our families, God is not simply an abstract idea, a "Force."

Families also teach us how to get along with people. It's one thing to make friends at work or at school, and quite another to survive day after day with family members, sharing a bathroom or a bedroom, doing chores, accepting parents' discipline. On that basis, parents' faults come out. Your brother's faults come out. Everyone's faults come out. It is not easy to love each other.

Yet relationships are the key to life. It is for loving each other, not for great miracles, that Jesus said Christians will be known. It is relationships—in church, at home, at work—that Paul constantly stressed in his writings. And one very personal relationship, to God, is the foundation of our lives.

Families rub off our rough edges. They teach us how to compromise; we can't always get our way. They teach us how to take orders; our parents are not the last authorities we'll be under. They teach us, ideally, the meaning of love,

especially in situations where love is not really easy.

Families aren't supposed to be easy. We're not meant to live free from friction; it's the friction that rubs off the edges. It is inevitable that, in growing into adults, we feel some tension and some pain.

Even a bad family usually teaches more than no family at all. It is a rare family that will totally dump you for misbehaving. Your family will not fire you the way some future boss may, or drop you as a friend the way someone at school may. Families, even bad families, normally hang on to their members, continuing to feed and clothe them. And most families provide some kind of loving support, so that the pain of rough edges can be tolerated.

Granted, your family has faults. But what strengths does it have? Aren't you much better off than you would be with no family at all?

I believe firmly that with better communication and a strong will to make things better most families can improve. They will not improve, however, as long as you focus only on the problems. The problems should only be a starting place; the focus should shift toward positive qualities. For instance, rather than complaining about arbitrary rules all the time, as though you preferred no rules at all, you could concentrate on working toward a set of rules that would encourage you to be disciplined yet also show respect for everyone involved.

Even if you can't change your family situation, its positive qualities deserve your attention. The worst thing you can get from a less-than-perfect family is a negative attitude toward life. If at eighteen or twenty-one you leave your family with a list of all the terrible things that were done to you, you will probably end up doing the same things to other people. If all you think about is how narrow your parents' minds were, your own mind will probably develop its own kind of narrowness.

But if you leave your family with a list of qualities that make a family relationship (or any relationship) ideal, you are headed *toward* something, not simply away from something. You are headed toward just the kind of maturity that families were designed by God to produce.

"Come on, Dad! Do you have to do this with all my dates?"

What My Parents Did Right

Campus Life Editors

Every family has its problems. And every parent makes mistakes. Sometimes we forget that they also do much that is right. To highlight the positive, the Campus Life *editors recall some of the qualities they gained from their parents. These families were no more perfect than yours. But they passed on some qualities worth remembering.*

Appreciation

When I was in high school, I lived in a trailer—a rectangle of tin and fake wood paneling ten feet wide and forty-eight feet long. My brother and I slept on bunk beds, which, when pushed against the wall, allowed us just enough room to dress if we took turns. Because there was no trailer park within ten miles of us, we rented a space on someone's private lot. We were the only ones in our school who didn't live in a house or apartment building.

No one in my school knew where I lived; I never had classmates over. When I caught a ride home after some school activity, I invariably directed the driver to a friend's house around the block. I strolled casually toward

Eugene's house, turned and waved, and, as soon as the car disappeared, scaled Eugene's fence and cut through a field to our trailer.

That procedure stands out because it was one of the only times I felt poor. Although my mother, a widow, brought home an income well below the official poverty level, and I never knew the luxury of an allowance, she somehow instilled in us a sense that our appreciation for life did not rise or fall with the total in her checking account. We had good food, a clanky piano to practice on, a faithful dog, a basketball hoop without a net, and a thirty-acre forest to explore next door.

Many parents spend long hours with lawyers, huddled over investment papers, trying to decide the best way to arrange their will for the sake of their kids. I wonder, though, how many of them spend equal time deciding what attitude toward money they will bequeath. Is money an almost sacred goal worth working overtime every night to acquire? Is it a cheap way of expressing love for parents who shrink from more personal means of expression?

Never once while growing up did I feel rich. But seldom did I feel poor, although by all objective standards we deserved that label. Somehow (I'm still not quite sure how), my mother taught me that my worth had nothing to do with piles of green bills or stock certificates stashed away in some dresser. My inheritance is one I will never deplete.

—*Philip Yancey*

Flexibility

"But Mom," I whined, "What's the big problem? All the other kids wear their hair long nowadays!"

I sat on a rickety metal stool in the upstairs

bathroom with a tattered bed sheet around my neck. Mom was about to cut my hair, and I didn't want her to. When I was in high school, long hair was "in," and short styles like mine often invoked chuckles.

"Verne," Mom replied, "You are not 'all the other kids.' You're a part of our family, and you live by our rules." She reached to plug in the electric hair clippers.

My parents were pretty conservative Christians—more conservative than I was at the time, anyway. Sometimes they seemed overly concerned about appearances—as if there were a "Christian" hairstyle or outfit. I was only a young Christian myself, having committed my life to God at a Campus Life meeting. But one of the strong messages I received from reading the Bible and from talking with older Christians was that a Christian was changed on the *inside*, and that the inside was what really mattered, not the outside. I had even heard my parents tell me that.

So I took a chance and tried the line on Mom: "But you and Dad tell me that for a Christian what's in the heart is what counts, right? You guys know that I'm not a rebellious kid, don't you? A little hair over my ears isn't going to damage my morals."

There was a brief pause. Mom sighed. "Well, I'm still going to trim a couple spots where your hair is sticking out," she conceded with a brief smile. "And I still have to see at least the bottom half of those ears."

The clippers buzzed for a minute or two, but I didn't care. I admired Mom for her willingness to keep learning and growing, even as I was.

On numerous occasions I have seen my

parents continue in that pattern of openmindedness; I've watched them realize that the way they've "always" done things isn't always the best (or only) way. I only hope that I can maintain that same desire to keep growing, learning, and adapting to new ideas.

—*Verne Becker*

Hospitality

Lula Mae Blackwell was not your typical neighbor. She and her husband T.W. lived in a two-room tenant farmhouse in the middle of a cotton field, just a stone's throw from our cow pasture.

Every morning when T.W. headed for the fields, Lula Mae walked up the road to visit the neighbors. The problem was we were the only neighbors within walking distance.

"Here comes Lula Mae," one of my brothers would yell from the front window.

"Not again," I'd groan.

But sure enough—she'd soon be walking in the front door without knocking, followed by her sweaty scent, which permeated the air.

Lula Mae talked nonstop; it didn't matter if anyone else was speaking. She didn't notice. She would have been better off had she never opened her mouth, partly because she never had anything to say and partly because her mouth was an unpleasant mosaic of tobacco-juice stain and tooth decay.

While talking, Lula Mae shuffled around Mom's polished wood floors in floppy brown boots that left trails of topsoil wherever she went. When she got tired of following Mom around, Lula Mae plopped down her 230 pounds between the delicate arms of Mother's antique Boston rocker. And there she would vigorously rock her morning away while she talked and waited for lunch to be served.

"She's a leech," I complained to Mom one day after Lula Mae left.

"But she's lonely," Mom responded. Every day I hoped Lula Mae would forget to come. But she never did. And every day my mom welcomed her with a smile, served her tea in the best teacup from the china closet, and, at lunch time, dished her up an extra bowl of soup. That has always stuck in my mind. Today, when I'm tempted to spend time only with those I like best, those who are just like me, I remember Lula Mae, my mother, and lonely people.

—Ruth Senter

Concern

I stood in front of the mirror, brushing my teeth and daydreaming about an upcoming date. My dad stepped into the bathroom. Mom stopped in the hall outside the door.

"There's something we want to talk about with you," Dad said. A tone of hesitancy in his voice hinted at the seriousness of his mood.

"Your mother and I are very concerned about your relationship with Dawn," Dad began. "You seem to be getting serious so soon."

I responded quickly and a little too loudly. "I'm not getting serious."

"We're glad to hear that," Dad said. "But I hope you understand our concern. You're a high school senior; you've never dated much. Suddenly you meet Dawn and you're with her all the time. Do you understand how it looks from our perspective?"

I knew they were especially concerned because Dawn wasn't a Christian. "Yeah," I admitted. "But you have nothing to worry about."

"We just don't want to see you get hurt by making some big mistake," Dad said as he turned to leave.

I never had seen any long-range future for my relationship with Dawn. But I've often wondered how much that talk with my parents affected my decision to explain my feelings to Dawn. (We broke up a few months later.) At the least, my folks' willingness to express their concern helped strengthen my own resolve not to get too involved.

Thinking back on that scene, I appreciate the positive approach my parents took. They didn't order me to cool things with Dawn. That would have made me more defensive, angry, and perhaps determined to maintain the relationship. Instead they emphasized their concern and expressed their feelings.

Their concern for me didn't surface only when they were worried about something like a dating relationship. My parents always took a personal, time-consuming interest in every area of my life. I appreciate their concern even more now than I did then.

—*Gregg Lewis*

Sense of Humor

I'll never forget the April Fool's Day we spent with another family at a cottage in northern Wisconsin. The deep drifted snow was frozen solid on the surface. We kids could walk on it, but the heavier adults would take a step, break through and plunge to their waists. This was comical to watch and it gave my mother a great idea.

She called several of us children to the back of the cabin and described a devious plot that called for us to feign an emergency down on the lake so she could arouse the two sleeping fathers and then watch them charge down the hillside through the ice-coated snow. Since the ice on the lake was beginning to break up, it was the perfect setting for a bona fide crisis. In a few moments, we were in our places down on the lake and Mom gave the cue.

"Help . . . help!" we screamed. "Mark fell through the ice! Dad . . . help . . . somebody!" In a flash, both fathers came bounding out of the cabin and started charging down the hill. With each step they'd rest a foot on the frozen surface, but when their weight shifted—crunch—they'd crash through. And so it was all the way down. Step . . . steady . . . crunch . . . crash! Step . . . steady . . . crunch . . . crash! It was hilarious! And so were the looks on their faces once they'd finally struggled to the bottom and we announced in chorus, "April Fools!"

My parents considered pranks, laughter, and a sense of humor essential ingredients for a family. And that fun-loving attitude not only made growing up more bearable, it provided a host of great memories. Even now, whenever our family gets together, we spend time laughing together as we rehash old stories and memories of the fun times.

I'm grateful for my parents' love of life and their subtle urging to take God more seriously, but myself and everyday life less seriously.

—*Scott Bolinder*

Protection

I remember the day my father arrived home with a small Sunfish sailboat strapped to the roof of his car. "Dad, Dad, what is it? Is it mine?" I threw my arms around his big shoulders.

"You *know* what it is," he said, engulfing me in a great hug. "And she's yours."

My lessons began the next day. Dad insisted that I do *everything* myself. I cried in exasperation as I backed the stick-shift car with its snaky trailer down the boat ramp.

"Try again," he said. "I'm only coming till you get your license; then it's up to you."

Learning Dad's sailing lingo was even harder, though I had spent hours hanging around boats with him. My performance was poor, but Dad didn't hold me back. Within a very few days he had set me loose, giving me lenient boundaries (no further east than the port, as far west as I could see). He soberly reminded me of the rules: Keep my eye to the west for summer storms; stay with the boat in case of trouble; leave a note saying where I put off and when I'd return.

The next few summers were difficult for me socially. Many of my friends seemed to live for parties and dancing in local hangouts I was seldom allowed to frequent. I chafed at what I felt were overly protective restrictions.

Not surprisingly, sailing became my refuge. And after being on the water all day, I was too tired to argue with much fervor about not being able to party with my friends. Besides, I wanted to be up and out as early as possible the next morning.

Dad cared enough about me as a person to not simply say "No!" to something I wanted to do. He gave me something better to replace it. In the face of mounting pressure from my peers, he handed me a gratifying and demanding skill to learn, one I'm still interested in.

"I was in that boat for hours," I told him last

year. "You could have been a lot more worried and afraid."

He laughed. And grinned his grin. "You don't know how many afternoons a little car was parked on the bluffs, with a father searching way down the horizon for a dot-of-a-boat with a blue and white sail," he said. "I had my eye on you more than you'll ever know."

—*Andrea Midgett*

Communication

When I started dating, I thought there was something wrong with me—bad breath, perhaps. Girls were just reluctant to go out a second time, especially if there was a meal involved. One girl finally leveled with me.

"Rick," she said, "it's just that you eat so slowly, and frankly, I don't have the patience. Last weekend, the waitress wanted to go home, the restaurant was closing, and you were *still* chewing. And when the manager started flashing the lights to give you a hint . . . I mean, how do you think that made *me* feel?"

"It's my parents' fault," I blurted out.

"Huh?"

I began to explain that as I was growing up my family never ate much before eight o'clock. My dad always called at 5:30 to say he was on his way home, a conversation that sometimes stretched to fifteen minutes with my mom asking how his day went.

When he finally arrived, he would hang up his coat and settle down on the living room couch. My mom would join him and they would talk some more. They talked freely about everything, and there wasn't anything they didn't seem to know about each other.

Trouble is, it always put dinner off a couple hours. And when we finally got around to eating, my parents wanted to talk to us kids, too. They would ask about school, our friends, teachers they knew, our homework. Dinner was never an eat-and-run affair.

Sometimes I wished my family's eating habits were more normal. When I ate at a friend's, everybody wolfed down the food in ten minutes and then had plenty of time to do their own thing. Their parents weren't so gabby— they understood that kids would rather have their privacy and not talk so much.

"So you see," I told the girl, "it's my parents' fault that I take all night to eat dinner. But I don't think they can change—they've been doing it that way for as long as I've known them."

"How long have they been married?" she asked.

"Thirty years."

It seems ironic. Her parents had split up five years before.

—S. Rickly Christian

A Tale of Two Sisters

Hope Warwick

A young father had two daughters.

As the years went by, he watched them grow up through watching "Sesame Street," roller skates, an awakening awareness of boys, and a bewildering series of diets. They teased each other, fought some, and increasingly took for granted their life together at 205 Woodfield Place.

One day, when the youngest was sixteen, she decided she could do without homework and curfews and the endless mother-daughter hassles over what to wear and who to go with.

So she stuffed an extra pair of jeans into her sleeping bag, cashed in two government bonds she'd been given to save toward college, and hiked about three miles down

136

an abandoned railroad track to the outskirts of town. At dusk, she cut across a vacant lot to the freeway and hitched the first of five rides between her Pittsburgh suburb and New York.

Police couldn't trace her. And every runaway organization her parents managed to contact could give no information.

In the city, she blew all she had on a one-month stint in a dingy hotel and on other unfun things like food, an extra blanket, a red nylon parka, and deodorant.

There was no homework.

When she ran out of money, a group of kids she'd gotten in with offered her a damp corner of their basement room.

She discovered that pot made her sick (dizzy, vomiting sick), and though it embarrassed her to no end, she never tried other drugs after that. She discovered, too, that these new transient friends used her as thoroughly and callously as the kids and teachers back home had seemed to.

Her sleeping bag got moldy.

For two weeks she wandered around downtown Manhattan, checking out "Help Wanted, Female" ads, but no luck. She bought a paper and sat down at one of the back booths of a greasy pizza joint to read more ads. Her feet hurt; both heels were blistered. She had a headache.

She thought about the dark, eight-block walk to her corner room, and decided she was going home. So she called her dad, and he wired money for plane fare, even for a taxi to the airport, though she told him she could take a bus.

Early the next morning on board U.S. Air flight 841, she reclined her seat as far as it would go and slept deeply.

At the terminal, her dad waited, straining to see her in the crowd as she emerged from the gate. He greeted her with a hug, and even as they walked the long concourse he did not once accuse her of hurting him. She knew he never would.

Out in the parking lot, he led her to an '85 Toyota.

"You've come down in status," she said. "Did you sell your Buick?"

"No. This one's yours." He gave her the keys and hugged

her hard. He was trembling, and she could recall having seen him so deeply moved only once before: when her mom came out of surgery and they said it wasn't cancer. "It could probably stand a paint job, but we thought you needed something to get around in."

Twenty minutes later, she pushed open the back door and walked into the warm, coppery kitchen. Bacon was frying, and the coffee was fresh-brewed.

Her sister slipped quietly into the family room, turned on the TV, and sat waiting for the test pattern to fade into an early morning talk show. She felt cheated, pushed aside. The happy reunion chatter in the kitchen ground into her stomach. What did all her attempts at being an ideal daughter mean anyway?

A few minutes later, when her dad came in to call her to breakfast, the nagging hurt inside her spilled out. "Okay, I don't claim to be perfect, but at least I've stayed home and done darn near every cruddy thing you've ever asked, and you never even say, 'Thank you.' I slaved in a restaurant to buy *my* car. Now *she* comes dragging back—a washed-out little streetsleeper who's blown her college savings and put you through hell, and you—you're *glad!*"

Her father stared at her for a long time, as though willing her to understand. "Our love for you is stronger than ever. But it's a time for joy! Your sister's back. If we couldn't forgive each other, we'd have no home."

Aspects of this story sound familiar? See Luke 15:11–32.

On My Own

Miller Clarke

Standing in front of the dorm, under a maple tree that was just starting to change color, I waved and watched my parents' car pull out into the street, stop at the end of the block, and then disappear around the corner. Ironically, at that very moment of freedom I'd dreamed about for years, I was nearly overcome by the urge to run down the street after that blue Pontiac and scream, "Don't leave me!" Instead, I turned and walked slowly, reluctantly back to my new room, my new life.

I was on my own. My parents were gone.

As I unpacked in my room, the memories of a lifetime flashed through my mind. And I remembered another "first day."

I'd said no one needed to walk me to the bus. I was finally a kindergartner; I was big enough. But as I waited at the corner, uncertainties overwhelmed my anticipation. And

139

before the bus arrived, I ran across the street and into a church to hide.

A few minutes later, as I hunkered down between two pews, I heard the church doors creak open and my mother's voice calling my name.

I expected a scolding. But instead, she took me to school herself and waited patiently by the door until I felt at ease. Then she slipped away.

Vacation time. I was fourteen. Dad and I were fishing for trout on the Yellowstone River, carefully wading along a shallow gravel bar, almost to the middle of the river. As we eased our way downstream, the water gradually deepened, and by the time we reached the end of the gravel bar, the water was waist deep and much too swift for us to work our way back upstream. So we plunged straight across the current toward shore. I was still a long way from the bank when I stepped in a hole, lost my balance, and felt the shock of ice water flowing over the top of my waders. But before the river could drag me downstream into deeper water, I felt my dad's hand grab the back of my shirt, and together we stumbled to shallow water near the shore.

It was only then, when the danger was past and the pounding in my chest subsided, that I realized what could have happened if Dad hadn't been right there.

The regional tournament. Basketball play-offs. Standing at center court before the opening tip, I scanned the crowd, looking for two faces among the thousands. And there they were, halfway up, behind the scorer's table.

I played more than a hundred high school basketball games. Mom and Dad missed maybe three. We shared a few thrills of victory and even more agonies of defeat.

All day long, as I unpacked my boxes and put my stuff in drawers, I kept remembering other times when Mom and Dad were there for me. I could see their faces in the hospital the night I broke my arm. I could remember Mom's loving smile as she brought me a cold glass of lemonade while I mowed the lawn one August afternoon. I could see my dad sitting in the car, as he had countless times, waiting to drive me home after ball practice.

And when I forced myself back into the reality of that dorm room, I found myself wondering if my new roommate could see *his* parents in every book, every piece of clothing *he* unpacked.

But that wasn't the kind of question you asked the first day you met someone. Maybe later.

By nightfall I had everything unpacked. Half a dozen drawers and one closet held the essential remains of eighteen years of life. But the crowded space seemed somehow empty. Even with a roommate, I felt very alone.

I didn't think eleven o'clock would ever come. But when it did, I walked to the phone booth at the end of the hall and placed my call.

On the third ring, Dad answered.

"Just wanted to make sure you and Mom got home okay," I said.

"Oh, sure," he said. And I could tell he knew the real reason I'd called. "Got in just a little while ago. Only took us about eleven hours."

Mom picked up the extension, and I told her I'd gotten everything unpacked and organized. And after she asked what I'd eaten and warned me to "eat right to keep your strength up," I told them I really needed to get back and hit the sack.

"You know we love you," Dad said.

"I know. I love you both, too."

When I hung up, it hit me. After twelve years of school, I was on my own. But after eighteen years of family, my parents weren't really gone. They were still there, just five hundred miles away.

With that thought I turned and walked back down the hall to my new room, my new life.

DINNERTIME
Mark Littleton

Grace is said. The food is passed. And Dad starts the conversation.

"What happened at school today?"

"Nothing" (my sister).

"Nothin'" (my brother).

"Nuttin'" (me).

Three nothings, with declining English. Three mental midgets.

I slip some peas down to the hidden hound stationed at my feet. Mom kicks me.

"What did I do?"

"You know."

My brother says, "Guess what Craig did today?" He tells us, with full comedic pathos and melodrama. Everyone roars. Dad tells us about his lunch last week in Japan, how he barely escaped having to eat a fish eye.

"I was staring at that eye, and it was staring back at me." More laughter. Mom tells about something the dog did. We giggle.

Then Dad starts in on the president, the economy, and a war somewhere. We yawn and fidget. Then he relates it all back to when he was a kid, with a clincher: "And let that be a lesson to you—a fool and his money are soon parted." We store it away for future reference for our kids.

My brother says, "May I be excused?" Mom nods. My sister says, "Good dinner, Mom." Dad grunts. I ditto. We all amble off

142

to hobbies, studies, dishes, TV, and occasional chuckles in the night, our bellies full.

Being a family has once again proved to be a success against all odds.

"From what *I* understand, his mother asked him to take out the garbage."

Mom, I've Outgrown You

Ann R. Eddy

At age sixteen I was three inches taller than my mother. We had a joke between us during that time. Since daughters usually end up taller than their mothers, we reasoned with mock seriousness, mothers must surely shrink.

During my freshman year at college I began to wonder if my mother hadn't shrunk mentally as well. By the time I came home for the Christmas holidays I realized that not only could I reach kitchen shelves Mother couldn't touch, but my mind, too, was exploring heights toward which she'd never stretched.

Over the next three years of school I became unhappily aware of a wider and wider gap between us. We couldn't agree on religion, politics, academic freedom, or what goals one should aim for in life. Our polite talks often exploded into hot arguments.

When I thought of Mother's sacrifices that let me get where I was, I would nearly weep. I had turned into the kind of daughter I thought I'd never be—one whose seeming ingratitude was breaking her parents' hearts. I finally vowed to bite my tongue rather than argue with Mom again.

All went well for three years and several short visits. Mom and I had never discussed the no-argument plan, but it was as though we both knew the rules perfectly. Most old subjects were taboo, and we carefully avoided new, potentially explosive subjects. Unfortunately, we were acting more like polite acquaintances than mother and daughter, and our relationship was becoming shallow and sad.

In the fourth year of our delicate truce, my husband was to present a paper at a medical convention, and this seemed a good time for me to spend a few days with Mom and Dad. Within an hour of my arrival, Mother and I had exchanged all the "safe" news. Three days of small talk loomed ahead.

Two of my mother's friends came for lunch that first day. I hadn't seen them in years, and so for a while I enjoyed their light chatter. But four hours of talk about grandchildren, the weather, and African violets exhausted me. I was annoyed, too, when they assumed that their rather slick, neat views on more complex subjects would naturally be mine as well.

When she finally closed the front door on her departing guests, my mother said to me, "Honey, you didn't have much to say. I do wish you had talked a little more."

"Mother," I burst out, "I didn't talk because I was bored! Don't you see that you and I have nothing in common? You either don't approve of or you don't understand everything I find worthwhile!"

I was shocked to hear my dark anger pour out. I sank into a handy chair. Mother sat down more slowly, as if she were bravely sustaining an arrow through her heart.

But when she spoke it was as if she had read my old thoughts. "You've outgrown me, Ann," she said evenly. "It's hard for a mother to accept, but you have, and I think it always happens. I outgrew my mother. When I was your age I'd go back home to the farm and think I was going to scream from boredom. No one ever talked about anything but the crops; no one ever asked anything but 'How are your hens laying?'

"And once, in a very regrettable moment, I told my mother that she and Papa were dull and old-fashioned. Mama sat down with tears tracing the deep wrinkles of her cheeks and said, 'But, Nancy, that's because you've outgrown us. Papa and I raised you with the hope that you'd do things and learn things we never had the chance to do or learn. Our sacrifices have nurtured the very growth that's made you find us dull.' And then Mama said slowly, but with a strange pride, 'I reckon your feelings are proof of our success.'"

This was one of those crystal moments in life when you see yourself as part of an endless chain. This time it was a chain of mothers and daughters winding back through untold generations, every child outgrowing her mother by a little or a lot, only to make sacrifices for her own child and be outgrown herself.

Perhaps Mother and I saw the same chain, because the old chasm between us miraculously filled. For the first time in years we stood on solid, communicable ground. Our first exchange, I must say, wasn't very articulate. I found myself with my arms around my mother as we gave soggy comfort through our tears. In the days that followed, the easy warmth of those moments held fast.

Slowly we began to tackle those points of disagreement that had separated us over the past several years. Now the air was clear. The urgency was gone. We were willing to compromise, to admit agreement when we saw it, to acknowledge a good point on the other side, and most of all to listen.

We ended up still disagreeing about quite a few things. But our eager, open talks had shown me a wisdom in my mother I'd never acknowledged before.

By the next summer my dear mother had died. We had parted in love and respect. I knew I was what I was because of her. And I knew she had known that.

Why I Like My Parents

Tim Stafford

Somewhere between junior high and high school I became a very private person. I did not like to tell anyone what I did, who my friends were, or how well I was doing in school. I especially didn't like to tell my parents. I chose a quiet form of rebellion—of saying, "It's my life, and I'll choose whether to let you inside."

Consequently, from the time I was in the ninth grade all the way through college I never once showed my parents a report card. I wasn't ashamed—in fact, I was doing well. But I considered my grades my business and no one else's.

What amazes me is that my parents never asked. They must have wanted to know. Sometimes they would comment that they learned more about what I was doing from reading the school newspaper than from talking to me. But they didn't press it.

They did not treat each member of my family that same way. My brother got incessant reminders and questions about his school progress. He needed them. I really didn't. And because I was allowed my own quiet form of rebellion, I never felt the need to rebel in more significant ways. I never had to smoke dope or run away to prove that I was different from the

147

rest of the family, because they always allowed me to be an individual.

But I'm not writing to gloat about my family, or make anyone feel jealous. I want you to think with me about what makes a family good . . . what made mine good, and what makes any family what it ought to be. Obviously, not every family should be like mine. Some things that suit us would bore other people to tears; we do things our own odd way. But underneath our oddness is a set of principles I think every family should have.

"Look, Mom and Dad, all I want is a little more independence. Is that too much to ask?"

Acceptance

When my parents didn't demand to see my report card, it wasn't because they *approved* of my silence. They *accepted* it. They knew I was an individual who would have to work out my problems in my own way. They accepted me for what I was.

Some parents rank their kids the way radio

stations rank the Top Forty. (Similarly, some kids have a "favorite" parent.) Not so in our family. There are four kids in our family, all very different, but there are no favorites. Nor are there black sheep. Some of us make friends more easily than others; some are smarter; some are better looking; some have accomplished more.

At school you're known by differences: "He's slower than his brother." Or, "She's the pretty one." But inside a family that should be unfamiliar terminology. You are accepted as a member of the family, no matter what you do or how you look. A brother or sister or parent may wish you would change, but they won't reject you if you don't. Your membership card to your family is simply the fact that you were born. You belong.

Love

Perhaps what strikes me most is how my mother would look at me, smile and say, "You are *such* a nice-looking boy. You look especially nice when you smile." Maybe I did look nice to her, but I think most people saw a scowling, pimpled mask. My mother didn't scold me for scowling; she encouraged me to smile. She told me how nice I looked, and there was probably nothing I needed to hear more. I *felt* very ugly.

She got no reward for encouraging me. I never put my arms around her and thanked her for saying that. At best I would act embarrassed and stalk off. At worst I would tell her in an irritated tone to leave me alone. But she never got tired of telling me how nice I looked when I smiled. She persistently loved me, even when I persistently refused her love. She was really the only person who kept me from feeling hopelessly ugly. She did it without reward, and she did it day after day after day. That is the quality of love you seldom find in a friend, but strangely enough often find in parents. Yet most of us wake up to our parents' love last of all.

Sacrifice

It's hard to think of an example of how my parents sacrificed for me—not because they didn't sacrifice, but because they did it so naturally, without thought. They never told us how much they were giving up for us. Sacrifice? I don't think they would have thought of it that way. It was just the way people act in a family.

They sacrificed money. They sacrificed time. They sacrificed their lives. They fed us, wiped our runny noses, held us when we were sick. They put up with our sophomoric, smart-alecky talk. They sent us to college. They might have had only two kids (or none) so they could live in a nicer house, be freer to go where they wanted on vacations, have some peace and quiet. Instead they had four of us. I'm not saying they got no rewards for their sacrifice—I know that they loved being our parents, even though it was a great pain at times. But with or without the rewards, they unhesitatingly sacrificed their own goals for the good of the family.

From a very early age they expected us to do the same. If the family was going on a picnic, it didn't matter that you had something you would rather do with your friends. A family picnic came before your personal desires. You, too, could sacrifice for your family.

Priorities

While they sacrificed for us, my parents also kept their priorities straight. When I was very small the subject of choosing between us kids and my father came up in a conversation with my mother. I can remember the shock. "I love you very much," my mother said. "And I can't imagine how the choice would ever come up. But if it ever did, I would have to go with Daddy. As much as I love you, I love him more." For a few hours after that I felt very small and lonely. But I always knew from that time on that my parents' relationship to each other came first.

So did their relationship with God. It was communicated in small ways. If my mother was praying in the morning, she would not stop to help me find my shoes. We *always* went to church on Sunday, even when we were on vacation.

Neither of my parents provided a taxi service for us. We lived quite a long way from school, so we often needed rides to school events. And they were glad to take us, when it was convenient. But they did not drop everything to cart us places. We would get rides from friends, or walk, or just not go. Was it because they didn't love us enough? They made it very clear in other ways just how much they did love us. But they also made it clear that their lives were not wrapped around ours. They did not exist to be our servants; we did not exist as theirs. They lived first for each other, for God, for the priorities (family included) that God had given them. Even though that meant I got deprived of a few things—help finding my shoes, or a ride to a meeting of the Math Club— I'm grateful for it. It provided me with a model for forming my own life. And it made it easier to leave my parents when the time came. They could happily see me go because I was not taking their life with me.

Discipline

There were rules. True, there were fewer and fewer rules as I got older, but there were always rules. If you disobeyed them you got punished. As I remember, I got punished a lot.

There were chores to do. It was *our* house, not "their" house where we kids happened to reside. Our parents were working hard to help us, and we were expected to work hard to help them. I don't remember this being a big deal. It was just expected, and we did it. Where it usually becomes a big deal is where it isn't expected, and kids get away with murder. Pretty soon they begin to think that the world exists to do them a favor. When they begin to find out that isn't so, it hurts.

Communication

There are many ways of communicating, and only a few of them involve the mouth. A hug may communicate more love than words. But words do a lot, too. There was always lots of conversation at our dinner table, and it was usually interesting. I remember, too, the late-night kitchen conversations with my mother, long after everyone had gone to bed. She would talk, and she would listen, too. Communication goes both directions.

A family can have the greatest love and respect and acceptance, but if they don't communicate that to each other, it all goes for practically nothing.

Faith

Maybe the best thing I can say for my parents is that each one of us four kids came to know Jesus Christ. That happened despite the fact—and maybe because of the fact—that my parents didn't push their faith. It was part of their respect for us. They required that we go to church, and there was plenty of talk about God in our house. But they were not uptight, the way it must be very easy for parents to be when they know just how crucial faith is.

I can remember vividly a period when, in high school, I was having grave doubts as to whether I was really a Christian. I didn't even know just what a Christian was, but I was sure that whatever a Christian was, my parents were. I could never deny Christ's reality in their lives. They were not religious fanatics, but they looked at the world—at their home, at their family, their jobs, their money, their children—from a Christian point of view. They were not uptight about any of it because they knew God was in control.

As you've read this list, I hope you've checked it off against your family. No doubt there are superficial things you both like and dislike about your family. You like the fact that you take vacations together. You dislike your parents' insistence on a midnight curfew. But how do you like your family when you talk about the qualities under the surface—love, respect, faith? Maybe you found as you read the list that you were saying, "My family is just as good as his." Or perhaps you found yourself wondering what you could do to change some areas where an important quality was weak or even missing.

Either way, it can do you good to think about it. These "underneath" qualities are what families are really for. There is no better place to learn them.

HOW TO GET THERE

So you understand something of how your parents feel—their fears and their love for you. You realize you aren't the only one with family problems. You even have an idea of what you'd like your family to become. But how do you get from here to there? Your parents make the rules. Can you change things?

The answer is, "Somewhat."

No, you can't be absolutely sure of changing your family. But yes, you can make a difference. In some situations—after a death or a divorce, or when someone is mentally or physically sick—you can't expect to make your family function ideally. Sometimes the difference you make will be simply to keep things from getting worse or falling apart. But at least you can help make things better than they are.

In other situations you can make a more positive difference. A single person willing to love can sway every other family member. It may take time, patience, and perhaps more personal strength than you now have. But what could be more worth the effort?

This section gives you practical strategies for moving your family closer to what it ought to be.

The Four Biggest Hassles

Jay Kesler

When I talk to kids who have problems at home, I usually begin by asking them what they don't like about their parents. I hear four complaints again and again:

My parents don't trust me.
My parents don't love me.
My parents don't listen to me.
My parents pick on me.

The problems exist, and they're not all your fault. Neither are they all your parents' fault. When people have trouble getting along, the problem usually has built up over time. You can't say, "One is at fault and one is innocent." Both sides are responsible.

Let's look at your end of the problem. It's the only end you can change.

My Parents Don't Trust Me

Many kids tell me their parents don't trust them. Their folks don't trust them to go on a trip, or take the family car somewhere, or choose their own friends. Those are liberties everyone wants to be trusted with—cars, freedom, friends. But how do you get to be trusted?

You have to be trustworthy, or "worthy of trust." You have to prove you deserve trust. You do it by starting with little things. If your parents give you curfews and you're always late, they're going to say, "Well, he can't tell time, so he certainly can't be trusted with something bigger." However, if you call from wherever and say, "Hey, Dad, I'm on my way, but it's going to take twenty-five minutes to get home, so I'll be ten minutes late," you'll find that when you want other privileges you'll have a chance.

There's a good reason behind this. If your parents are smart, their goal is for you to become independent. They don't particularly want baby birds in the nest forever. They want you to fly.

But to fly, you have to develop gradually. You don't go out and challenge the neighborhood cat the first day. You go out on little loops to see if you can do it. The loops get bigger and bigger; the day may come when you're ready for the neighborhood cat. When you're ready for something tough, your parents will enjoy it with you. But to get to that stage, you have to excel at the little loops.

Break down another word: Responsibility. It's "response ability," the ability to respond maturely to situations. Believe me, your parents watch how you respond to different situations. Do you respond to money maturely, or does it burn a hole in your pocket? When disappointed, do you take it in stride, or do you pout for a week? Parents watch, not to spy on you, but to check your response ability, to see if you're ready for more.

If you really want privileges at home, I'll tell you how to get them: Start doing all the little, dumb stuff, according to the book. Stuff like making your bed, picking up your clothes and being neat, doing the dishes without being hassled into it.

Parents are trainable. It's all in how you think of it. Like the two mice talking about the scientist. One mouse says to the other, "I think we've got the scientist conditioned. Every time I push this little lever he gives me food."

Another need: Communication. A kid told me, "My parents don't trust me with my friends. They don't like them because of their dress— they think they're troublemakers. If they knew what the kids they *want* me to hang out with are like, they'd be glad I have the friends I do."

"Have you ever thought of telling them?" I asked.

How can you expect your parents to trust you with your friends unless you've told them what your friends are like? If every time your parents ask you a question you grunt and make them feel like it's none of their business, they're not going to trust your friends.

Kids say, "My mom doesn't trust me."

"Why not?" I ask.

"Well, she reads all the papers and hears about all the things kids are doing, and she thinks that's what I'm doing."

"Well, does your mother know anything about you?"

"Not really."

"Why not?"

"I guess because I never told her."

Do you ever sit down and tell your parents what kind of person you are? What you want out of life? What your values are? As your parents see your ideas maturing, they will feel more confident to say, "He can be trusted when we're not here."

"Your father really *does* watch you like a hawk, doesn't he?"

My Parents Don't Love Me

When kids complain that their parents don't love them, I wonder how much they know about their parents.

I know what my mornings are like. Some people get up every morning and say, "Good morning, Lord." I tend to say, "Good Lord, morning."

Each morning I have conversations with the shower nozzle. From my state of semiconsciousness it looks like the only friendly thing in the world. I talk to it about my life and the day ahead. I say, "Man, I've got to go to work again, the same job I've been doing every day for seventeen years. There's no way out—it's a life sentence. The kids are eating more; utility rates are soaring; the more I make the more expenses seem to rise. Help!"

A million other parents do that every day. You think your father's trapped in the corporate jungle? You're probably right.

Why does he do it? He could jump in a car, start driving, and never come back. He could desert your family and run around conceiving kids like you. That's fun, you know: no responsibilities. Just how many pleasures does your father treat himself to? Probably not many.

So why does he stick to being your father? The only explanation that makes much sense is that he loves you, and he's determined to take care of you. Maybe he doesn't know how to show his love properly, but he does love you. His intentions are good.

What about your mom? Do you think she loves you? Before you answer, go to the cupboard, open the door, and look at all the dishes. Then start with the number of days in the year. Multiply that by the meals in a day. Multiply that by how old you are. That's roughly the number of times your mother has washed those glasses and plates. Think that gets a little boring?

Look at your clothes. How many times has your mom washed those same clothes? How many times has she folded the T-shirt you're wearing? (And she may do all this plus work full-time at an outside job.) Think that gets old? Why does she do it?

My Parents Don't Listen to Me

It's amazing that people who live together for years can have such a hard time making intelligent conversation. It works both ways. You should see parents when I tell them this is a complaint kids have. They're amazed. From their point of view, it's kids who won't listen to them!

It's hard to make good conversation. It takes creativity and effort. If you interacted with friends like you do with your parents, how many friends would you have?

Sometimes parents want to talk but they don't know how. They ask questions no one cares about. "How's school?" You know how to break them of that? Tell them what school is like. Say, "Well, we got there at 8:10 and stood around waiting for the bell to ring. At 8:15 it rang and we went to homeroom. We sat there for a half-hour and had the announcements and did this and that. Then the bell rang again and we went to math. We were taught all about . . ." Your parents will eventually get the idea that more creative questions might help conversation.

I tell parents to try not to ask questions that can be answered with a simple "Yes" or "Okay." Ask questions that say, "What do you think of?" "What is your opinion about?" The same goes for you when talking with your parents. Try this one-week experiment. Sit down and think up five suppertime conversations you can talk to your parents about. Then list two or three questions for each meal. "Hey, Dad, what do you think about this?" or "Mom, what's your opinion on that?" They'll answer; everyone has an opinion. You may know more about it than they do, but don't always correct them. You're not going to change them, anyway. Just listen. Ask, "Why do you feel that way?" or "How did you come to your opinion?" Don't make your parents always end up arguing with you.

Don't trap your parents into logic that proves them wrong. It only makes them say "No" automatically because they know you're trying to manipulate them.

Practice speaking in sentences rather than grunts. A sentence is easy enough to make. Get a verb, stick a noun in front of it, and you're in business. Sentences communicate thoughts. A grunt or an inflection only communicates an attitude, and you can't converse with an attitude.

Another way to get your parents to listen is to tell them once in a while that you need them. Tell them when you've failed. I know a guy who came within a hairsbreadth of being hit by a train in the family car. He'd been careless, and it scared him half to death. He was really shook. There was no damage, but you know what he did? He went home and told his dad about it. He didn't have to, but he did. It was his way of saying, "I make mistakes." In terms of relating to his dad, it was the smartest thing he ever did.

Writing home when you're on a trip is good, too. Even a collect phone call won't get a complaint out of most parents. Nothing warms a parent's heart like knowing their child is a little homesick. You might be able to get along without a phone call home, or you may think, "My friends will think I'm a baby if I call." But decide what matters most to you. Do you want your parents to know they're loved?

My Parents Pick on Me

I find that a lot of "picking on me" is caused by a lack of information. Parents want to know what's going on in their kids' lives. Many times kids don't volunteer it. What can a parent do but pick?

Maybe your parents are always picking on you about your friends because they don't know what kind of people they are. If Susie Jones, the girl your mother thinks you *should* take out, is a hypocrite, sit down and explain that to your mother.

Kids complain that their parents pick on them about school, when often kids haven't told their parents enough about it. Once you volunteer the information, the picking will diminish.

You can eliminate some kinds of picking by figuring out what petty things bother your parents. What irritates your dad? Maybe it's that you slouch at the table, or he doesn't like it when you play the stereo in your room loudly when he's watching TV. Well, is it worth it? Is it worth hassling over every day for the next two or three years? If you know your mother gets irritated when you don't respond the first time to something she says, why not give in and respond right away? Don't make war with your parents. It's not worth it.

Sometimes there are good reasons why parents pick on their kids. Ever ask them why they care so much about the clothes you wear? They may have some well-founded reasons. Is it possible that your mother knows something about life that makes her think twice about certain clothes? You might try asking her.

Parents also pick on their kids because they're afraid. They see their time as parents ending and they want to do everything they can to mold and shape their children while they can. They're afraid time is running out and they haven't been as good parents as they wanted to be. Or they're afraid of the dangers the world holds for young people—a world that may seem ominously different from the world they grew up in. They may even be afraid you're going to turn out more like them than they want you to be.

Whatever the cause of your parents' fear, it signals their concern. Picking and nagging may not be the best ways to show love. But remembering the motivation should make it a little easier to take.

Another reason your parents may pick on you is your independence. Some parents don't understand their children trying to get away from the formless blob called "family." Your parents probably don't understand why you're tired of being so-and-so's son or daughter. They think you don't like them; they don't understand that you're just trying to find your own identity.

When you want to be alone in your room, they think it's because you don't like them. When you don't feel like going where the rest of the family is going, they take it as personal rejection. When you want to move out and get an apartment, they think it's because you can't stand to be in the same house with them. They forget what it's like to be your age, growing into independence.

So remind them. Explain that you're trying to become an individual. Sit down and explain to them as patiently as possible that you love them, but that you have to be known for what you are, not for what they are. It may take them a while, but I think they'll understand you, especially if you lace your talk liberally with the statement that you love and enjoy them. Many parents who pick on their kids are seeking some kind of assurance. You want them to stop picking? Try giving them the assurance.

Parents Are Lonely

What I'm saying is this: Be fair to parents. Be at least as fair to them as you would be to any friend. You know how unsure you feel when you get around a group of people you don't know? Well, that's how parents feel around high school kids. They don't know quite how to act. Do you blame them?

I try to make some assumptions about everyone I meet. I think you can apply them to your parents, too, since they are people.

I always assume that everyone I meet is lonely. I won't always be right, but I'll be right about 95 percent of the time. I assume everyone is frightened and insecure, so I try to do things that won't threaten them.

What would it do to your relationship if you made the same assumptions about your parents? What if you made a special point of being nice when they were busy or uptight over something? What if you occasionally complimented them? Approach your mother some night when she's doing the dishes and give her a hug, not to try to get something out of her, but just to say you love her. It'll make little warm shivers go up and down her spine.

Lovers do things for each other simply because they want to—not because they hope to get something out of it. It makes them feel good to do it. There's a scriptural principle here, too. It's expressed beautifully in the famous prayer of St. Francis of Assisi, who said, "Grant that I may not so much seek to be loved as to love."

Real love isn't sentimental. You'll learn by practicing it at home.

Problem Parents

Sometimes parents have deep problems.

Most parents, I'm convinced, really love their kids and want to help them. But there are exceptions, and of course every parent has faults of some kind. How do you handle them?

Suppose your dad had only one leg. Would you be angry that he couldn't run races with you? Not a chance.

Well, suppose your dad or mom has been crippled psychologically by certain things in his or her youth. Will you hold it against them because, say, they were raised in homes where discipline was administered unwisely and they picked up the wrong signals, and now they overdo it with you? If your mom overreacts, could it be because something happened to make her fearful, something she'd never be able to talk about with you?

Will Rogers said he never met a man he didn't like. He didn't say that because he had the incredible fortune to meet only great people. He meant that if you get to know a person well enough, you can like him, and you can accept his flaws. That's true of parents, too. Why look only at the negatives? If your parents were someone else's, you would probably think they were interesting characters.

What's more, there's the possibility of learning from them. Most people learn from positive examples; that's certainly the easiest. But there is another possibility: to learn from negative examples.

I know a couple of guys who were raised in a terrible family situation. Their parents fought constantly, always threatening divorce. The two sons took very different paths. One got all involved in the situation. He jumped in the middle of the fights, taking one side or the other. The cycle got to him. You see, no matter how much you dislike your parents now, you'll find yourself acting just like them unless you do something about it. That's one of the worst things about a bad home: It creates a cycle that doesn't stop with one generation. That son ended up making the same tragic mistakes his parents made.

The other son, however, broke the cycle. He didn't get involved in the fights; he backed away and did his own thing. He helped when he could, but primarily, when things got bad he backed off. Today he's together. Why? Because he worked at learning from a bad situation.

Okay, your father is a drunk or your mother is an addict, or your folks are always fighting. It's a problem that can't be solved overnight, and if the persons involved don't want to change, it won't ever be solved. You're stuck with it, at least until you're eighteen and can make a life of your own.

But don't spend all your time blaming your parents. They're crippled in some ways. The best you can do is be kind. Just say to yourself, "When I get married I'm going to be a little more careful to find the right kind of mate," or, "When I have a son I'm going to be a better listener than my dad was."

That takes a lot of maturity. But it can be done.

It's tough to have a good relationship with your parents. Very few people are completely successful at it. Every family has tensions and conflict. But a good relationship with your parents can make a tremendously positive difference. Few things are closer to you emotionally than your parents. When things are bad at home, everything is affected. And when things are good at home, the world is a much happier place to be.

Strategies for When You Disagree

Gregg Lewis

Slowly, silently you open the front door. Hoping against hope, you plot the quietest course from the front door through the darkened house to your bedroom. But as you tiptoe down the hall past your parents' room, your dad calls out your name and inquires, "Do you know it's forty-five minutes past your curfew? Where have you been?"

It's the second time you've been late in the last two weeks. And you have no good excuse. Basically you just lost track of time.

The brief discussion goes pretty much as you feared. Saying you're sorry obviously isn't going to be enough. But you are still distressed to hear your dad declare, "I don't want to hear any more tonight. But as of right now, you're grounded for the next month!"

Standing in the dark, at the foot of your parents' bed, a tidal wave of mixed emotions begins to churn inside you as you try to decide how to respond.

- "You're grounded!"
- "No, you can't go."
- "Rules are rules."

- "I don't care whose parents let them do it. We're your parents and we say no."
- "Of course you have to be back by ten. This is a school night."
- "You can't wear that to school."

"When I said, 'Get your *rear end* in here,' you knew very well what I meant, young man!"

All parents have their own expectations. And there probably hasn't been one teenager in the history of the world who didn't eventually crash head-on into some parental regulations or punishments. Every time a rule or a restriction is invoked, the question arises: "How will I react?"

There are a number of non-recommended responses:

- You can stomp out of the room and slam the door in protest.
- You can argue loudly, protesting that your parents are unfair.
- You can stage an Academy Award winning performance of that old favorite role of "Poor, persecuted me."
- You can whine and plead in your best beggarly fashion.
- You can cry and pout every time anyone looks your way.
- You can give your parent(s) a long dose of the silent treatment.

Sometimes one of these tactics will prompt your parents to give in. But because each of these responses actually attempts to turn the tables on your parents and punish them, they are more likely to increase their resistance. And none of these tactics will make it easier to settle a disagreement next time a confrontation arises.

So how *should* you react when you disagree with your parents' rules or restrictions? There's a lot that could be said, but you could divide the best advice into four steps.

1. Get Control.

One of the surest ways to maintain control of your response is to delay it. Allow yourself time to cool down and rein in your emotions. Express your feelings out loud when you're alone. Talk to yourself. Or better yet, talk to God. Sometimes writing down your feelings helps put them in perspective.

Think through and plan your response. Identify your feelings. Ask yourself what you want and expect to accomplish by questioning your parents. Decide what you're going to say and when. It often helps to remind yourself of your parents' motives. Most rules and restrictions arise out of genuine love and concern. Very, very few parents want to harass or deprive their kids.

2. Pick Your Time.

Once you've had a chance to cool down and gain control of your feelings, the question of timing may answer itself. Sometimes the best course of action is simply to abide by a rule, especially one you just violated. After a restriction or punishment is invoked is usually the worst time to discuss it.

The best time to negotiate on a rule is long before a situation arises. Reason is more apt to prevail in a hypothetical discussion, when emotions aren't involved.

But if you decide to disagree, look for a time when your parents are in a calm, receptive mood. If you can wait until you've just had some positive interaction with them, your chances will be better.

3. Confront with Care.

Once you've gotten control, decided your course of action, and carefully picked an opportune time, you still have to face your parents. And this is the trickiest step.

The tone of your approach is crucial. Don't demand, rave, or act defensive. If you can keep your feelings low-key, it will be easier for your parents to do the same. And the chances of a reasonable discussion will be greatly improved.

Two valuable communication strategies may really help are: active listening, and I-messages.

Don't just give your arguments and reasonings. Listen to what your parents have to say.

Listen attentively. Ask for clarification. Try to understand not only the reasons but the feelings behind them. And reflect back on what your parents say with words like this: "I hear you saying you feel . . ." or "In other words, you're concerned about . . ." Let them know you are genuinely trying to understand them.

And when you talk, use I-messages rather than you-messages. For example, instead of saying, "You don't trust me," say, "I feel as if you don't trust me." If you focus your comments on your own feelings, it'll sound a lot less like criticism and your parents won't feel as defensive.

4. Don't Just Talk.

If you hope to do further negotiating in the future, the best strategy is to show good faith by your actions. Observe and abide by the rules over a period of time and your parents will be likely to give you more leeway in making your own decisions.

But proving you are responsible will take more than obeying rules. Regularly watch for non-required things you can do for your folks without being asked. As time goes by they'll almost certainly notice and appreciate the effort.

The suggestions made here don't come with a money-back guarantee to get you whatever you want from your parents. You will most likely continue to have disagreements about rules and restrictions. But these guidelines will keep the conflict and the unpleasantness to a minimum.

WHEN YOUR PARENTS DON'T BELIEVE

Steve Lawhead

I magine this: You are growing up in a very poor family. Stone broke and destitute, you are making it day-to-day the best you can. But cold, hunger, and sickness are never far off. You see your mother and father (and siblings) tightening their belts and facing the bleak future without much hope of relief. You wish you could do something to help them, but you're as hungry as they are.

One day a very rich and generous man gives you a fortune—free, no strings attached. He does it because he likes you and wants to help. Suddenly you're rich—filthy rich, unspeakably rich. You'll never have to worry any more. So the first thing you do, naturally, is run home and tell your family the good news. Their poverty is over! Better days are ahead! Only, when you get home and display your new wealth, they all act like you're crazy or something.

Your father says, "I don't want anything to do with your funny money. Don't let me catch you with it around here any more!" Your mother says, "It's fine for you, dear. But I can't accept any of it—not now. Maybe someday I'll find a treasure, too." Your brother and sister say the same thing, "So what? Why make such a big deal out of nothing?"

No one understands. Instead, they grimly go on day after day as deep in debt and poverty as ever before. All your treasure is worthless to them.

How does that make you feel?

If you are a Christian and your parents aren't, you already know how that feels. You live that imaginary story every day in real life. No wonder a Christian kid's home life can often be an unsavory blend of pressure, frustration, and loneliness. How do you cope?

The loneliness a Christian feels living in a non-Christian family comes from the fact that communication on many levels is cut off. You don't feel free to share some of the most important things happening in your life. Often there is no support for your faith, no encouragement—two things every Christian needs.

When you don't get something at home, you go looking for it outside. You go to Bible studies, to prayer meetings, to Campus Life or Young Life club. You spend as much time with your Christian friends as possible. But this is where most young Christians should step lightly because too much living away from home makes parents feel abandoned.

Look at it from their point of view: Everything was fine until you became a Christian, and then, *bam*! Suddenly home isn't good enough for you and you'd rather spend all your time with your Christian friends. "What did we do?" they ask.

Anyone in this situation must continually look for new ways to share with his or her family. You can't read the Bible or pray together, but there are still many things you can do with your family. What did you do with them *before* you were a Christian? It's a good thing to keep in mind that your family has needs that can be filled only by *you*.

Loneliness is a two-way street. It could be your parents are lonely, too, now that you're a Christian. If you want support and encouragement from your family, it's best to keep the home fires burning. You can't expect your parents to support something that's taking you away from them. If anything, they'll try to discourage it to get you back.

"I'm not allowed to express *anything* in my family—love, hate, joy, anger, or anything," says Nancy, a high school senior. "My parents are not Christians and the atmosphere in our home is totally stifling. It's hard to maintain my enthusiasm as a Christian. I love my parents a lot, and I've shared the gospel with them, but they both have neat little arguments I can't break through.

"Dad says it's too easy—that problems aren't solved just by praying a little prayer. So he won't accept it. He wants everything written out and explained down to the last detail before he'll consider any of it. My mother thinks that if she just goes to church it's enough. They both think I'm strange; they think I'm turning into a fanatic because I pray out loud sometimes."

Nancy faces the same frustration many people do—of trying to relate a new life-style to an old family way of life. Buoyed up by all kinds of new feelings and sensations, Nancy wants to share them with her family, tell them why she's changing and how they can change, too. She feels stifled and frustrated when they don't respond.

It's easy to get frustrated when things don't work out the way you'd like. The only antidote to frustration is patience. Changes, especially major life changes, take time. Parents need time to think about what you're telling them. They have probably been thinking, feeling, and acting the way they do for a long time, and you want to upset the applecart altogether. Changing for them is just not as easy as it is for you.

A parent has to overcome a certain amount of skepticism before following in your footsteps. Remember, they've seen you go through many changes—from milk to solid food, from grade school to junior high, from a person who hates the opposite sex to one who can't stand being at a distance. They've also seen you take up fads and begin hobbies that lasted a month. How do they know this isn't one more fad? Christianity may be on your top ten today, but what about tomorrow? They need to see some stability in you before they can trust their lives to what you're saying. That takes time. But it's time that can be well-spent living your faith before them every day (rather than preaching at them), building yourself for the day when they start taking your new interest seriously.

Mark, a student from Seattle, became a Christian and immediately decided to use a direct approach on his family. He came home and preached to them, saying, "Repent! You're going to hell!" His new faith was met with outright hostility. His parents pressured him to give up preaching or leave home.

It doesn't take much insight to see that Mark's method lacked finesse. But for some reason many new Christians think that's the only way to share their faith. While it might catch people's attention, it usually only makes them mad. Put yourself in your parents' place. How would you like it if the person you've loved and cared for over the years came home one day and started telling you your whole life had been a waste, and you had better get it together because you're doomed? The baby whose diapers you changed now informs you that he knows the only true way to live, and everything you've taught him has been wrong. You'd get a bit hostile, too.

Mark was ingenious though. When he saw his first method wasn't working, he cooled it and switched to another technique. He subscribed to a Christian magazine and began reading it himself and leaving it lying around the house in strategic places. Then he waited. Mark never caught anyone reading his magazines, but he was suspicious. So he carefully placed them on a dusty table and checked for fingerprints. Sure enough, it was plain that his magazines were being read by his parents, and soon they began asking questions about what he believed. Then he was able to share with them in a way that made much more sense.

He also tried to be more loving and considerate. He offered to chip in and do chores without being asked. He spent time talking with his parents about everyday things and showed them affection regularly. That gave his parents a chance to see actions behind Mark's words.

As a result, Mark felt less pressure from them because he became less of a threat. The pressure you feel as a Christian in your own home may be related to the way you treat your family as non-Christians.

Jesus warned those who would follow him that he represented a divisive factor in their lives. "Do you think I have come to bring peace on earth?" he asked them. "No! Rather, strife and division. From now on families will be split apart, three in favor of me and two against, or perhaps the other way around. A father will decide one way about me; his son, the other; mother

BUSINESS REPLY MAIL

FIRST CLASS PERMIT NO. 8182 DES MOINES, IA

POSTAGE WILL BE PAID BY ADDRESSEE

CAMPUS LIFE
Subscription Services
P.O. Box 11624
Des Moines, IA 50347-1624

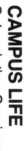

and daughter will disagree . . ." (Luke 12:51–53). Jesus knew what problems his life would bring to families.

Jesus knows and understands what you're going through. He, perhaps better than anyone else, can comfort you and help you deal with the pressure, frustration, and loneliness you feel as the only Christian in your home. And, happily, through time, patience, and endurance, he can also change things. But remember, he can never guarantee your parents will become Christians. That choice is theirs alone.

Bob tried in vain to get through the living room without showing his report card to his parents.

Midnight Writer

Name Withheld

The following letter is real (although the name has been changed). It was written on impulse at midnight by a high schooler—with no intention of its ever being published—as a means to grab her parents and cry out, "Look at me! This is the person I am!" Have you ever felt the same way Kathy does here?

Dear Mom and Dad:

I am writing you this letter because I have a lot on my mind that I want to tell you, and I know if I tried to say it in person I would either break up or get mad. Maybe I shouldn't write it, but I think I should let you know how I feel about things so we can understand each other better. The subject is our relationship to each other. Since I—not you—am writing this, it will be very one-sided, but here is how I feel.

Sometimes I picture myself as a dog on the end of a leash held by you, the masters. The dog struggles to get free, not because he hates his masters (actually he loves them and depends on them a great deal), but the fact that he is *tied* to them makes him want to get away. As time goes on, if he doesn't get free he will do almost anything, even bite his masters whom he loves.

You see me as a teeny-bopper adolescent who can't really feel and think yet. But maybe this isn't how you see me at all. I get the impression that you are so worried about how I will turn out that you will do anything to "protect me from myself." I feel that you want a stereotype for a daughter, not the real thing.

Do you want a "Susanna Goodwill"-type daughter? By this I mean a daughter who is nice, sweet, popular, and in high standing at the church youth group, and who never causes any problems because she and her parents agree on everything—and most important of all, if she has a boyfriend, he is her age and in the same youth group.

There is nothing wrong with this type, except it is not me. It never will be me! I am a person, not just your daughter. Don't you see that you are hurting more than helping? This brings us to the point of boyfriends. I am not looking for a husband. When I am interested in a boy, it is not because I want a romantic relationship. It is because I need a friend. You say that I have plenty of friends and friendship leads to deeper things. Maybe I just need someone to say, "I'll accept you as you are. You don't have to change for me." Maybe I just need someone I can talk to and share things with. Some friends you can share some things with and others you can share totally separate things with. Maybe I just need to be told, "Hey, I like you! I enjoy *being* with you. It doesn't matter what people say because I like you anyway."

I don't think any person finds total acceptance at home. That is why we tell things to our friends that we would never tell our parents. That is also why there is a generation gap; we just can't accept each other as we are. You are always trying to improve me. Do you realize how few times you say that I look nice? Sometimes, but that's only when I wear something you especially like, not that I like. (You could even lie a little, just to make me feel confident.)

If I'm not accepted by you, do you think that makes me more confident of being accepted by my friends? If you think I like John only because I am flattered he would even look at me, you're wrong. I care about him. From him I get this acceptance that is lacking here at home. I enjoy being with him. We understand each other. Hard as it is for you to believe, five years' difference in age does not make a whole lot of difference in people. Maybe I like being with him because I can relax and be myself with him. I don't have much hope that you'll change your minds, but this is how I feel.

Now I'd like to talk to you about church. On the retreat I gave my whole life back to God to do with what he wants.

I also learned that love is the greatest thing in the whole world. Undemanding, giving love. It's pretty easy to love my friends that way, but it's you I'm having trouble with. When I came in tonight, I really didn't expect to be so upset. I'll say again that I'm sorry if I hurt you (and I know I do with my thoughtless behavior). Do you think you could try letting go a little? That way you wouldn't get so hurt. I am the kind of person who must do it for herself, not take a more experienced person's word for it. Maybe I will get hurt but at least it will be because I made the mistake, not anyone else. I will be responsible for my own actions.

What a long letter this has turned into. It's past midnight. I hope you can not only read this letter but also read between the lines to get my meaning. I'm going to sign this the way I really feel, the way I have tried to express myself to you.
With much love,
Kathy

SOME IDEAS FOR CHANGE

Tim Stafford

When you discuss problems with your parents, you often communicate attitudes more than facts. How about suggesting one or more of these reforms?

Everyone needs privacy and a chance to think. Rooms should be private—parents' as well as kids'. If you want to go into someone else's room, knock or ask permission. Failing that, how about "Do not disturb" signs, or setting aside a "Quiet room" at certain hours?

For a week, try beginning every contradicting statement by saying, "That's your opinion, and I respect it."

Write out a workable compromise you can suggest to your parents on cars, money, chores, or hours. It saves fighting a fresh battle every time. And your parents are bound to be impressed if you suggest the rules in writing.

Set up a weekly/monthly family council. Alternate the leadership so that everyone can bring up the things that are bothering him or her. Make sure you include some positive things, too.

If things are really bad, suggest bringing in a third party—a respected adult, a pastor, or even a trained counselor to listen to your differences.

Revise schedules so everyone can fix one daily meal.

Agree to quit comparing. You won't compare your parents with other adults, your car and house with other cars and houses, your church with other churches—and your parents won't compare you with siblings, cousins, and friends, or compare your friends with other kids.

What God Can Do

Tim Stafford

When all is said about what you can do to affect your family, you can't do much.

You can make sure the problems aren't coming from your side. You can change your attitudes and do your best to understand whatever your parents' side of the problem may be. You can talk to your parents, propose some new ideas, try to explain how you feel about your conflicts. And you can take a large dose of patience, hoping that for these last few years at home you can survive your parents' faults, accepting them as human beings who make mistakes.

But you cannot make your parents change. They are unlikely to take much advice from you.

It is not even easy to change your own attitudes.

Powerful emotions constantly upset you (and them) when you try talking calmly to your parents. What starts out to be a rational discussion turns into slamming doors and shouting. Sometimes trying to make things better only makes them worse.

But what you can't do, God can. If problems with your parents do nothing more than make you start talking to God regularly, something good has already happened. The simple act of talking to God each day about your family situation may do more good than confrontations, family councils, counselors, and letters written at midnight.

God can help you keep your head straight. By praying every day, you renew your friendship with God, who loves you perfectly. You can feel totally secure in his love. You also remind yourself of what's really important. Instead of worrying yourself to death over conflicts with your mother, you remember that ultimately God is in control; what matters is obeying him, and living a life of love despite your circumstances.

You can specifically pray that God will help you keep your head straight by providing calmness to you, and by leading you to friends who can encourage you and strengthen your faith. You can pray that he will remind you of what is really important. If you do that, day after day, you are more likely to emerge from your family problems unscarred.

God can also directly intervene in your family. He can change attitudes and behavior. You can pray each day that he will work on the people involved—letting them know that he loves them, and helping them to be more secure, so they won't have to take out their fears and insecurity on you and each other. If your parents aren't Christians, you can pray that God will keep bringing himself to their attention.

But be warned before you pray: Usually God works *through* the lives of Christians. If you ask God to change something, chances are he will want to do it through you. If you ask God to affect your family, he will probably want first to affect you. Don't ask God for anything you aren't willing to work to get.

Be warned, too: God may not change your family. He

does not magically overhaul things whenever he is asked. Why not? Nobody knows for sure. But one thing is sure: It is through rough spots in families that God builds character. He teaches you patience. He teaches you how to get along when it's hard. He teaches you realism about yourself. He teaches you to rely on him. That hard lesson—reliance on him—may be the most important thing God can possibly give you. He cares about your relationship to your family, and he wants it to be better. But much, much more, he cares about your relationship to him.

Lorraine's worst nightmare comes true.

SECTION SIX

HOW ARE YOU DOING?

Now that you've read all about families, we'd like to put you to work. You need to develop a strategy for your own family. First comes evaluation, then action. There's real value in appreciating your family's strong points and working on the weak ones.

In this final chapter, we consider six qualities every family ought to have: Love, communication, respect, wholeness, discipline, and faith. For each, we ask a series of questions about your family. It will help if you jot down some answers as you go. Then, looking back over your responses, try to evaluate your family in each area. Do you need to work on it? Or is it a strong area, one you can be relatively satisfied with?

After each evaluation, you'll find a few practical suggestions. You can take these or add your own. (You might also want to flip back through the book and mark observations and suggestions that relate to your family's specific weaknesses.) You may wish to set some specific goals: one month, three months, and one year. The main point is: Don't just evaluate. Act.

A CHECKLIST FOR EVALUATION AND ACTION

Tim Stafford

Where is your family strong? Where is it weak?
LOVE

How many times a week does somebody say, "I love you"?

_____

_____

_____

How many times a week does somebody give a hug or other sign of love?

_____

_____

_____

Is any family member left out of these expressions of love?

_____

_____

_____

Draw your dining table with each family member in his or her place. Then draw lines indicating the relationships between all family members. For strong expressions of love, draw a double line. For moderate expressions, a single line. For hostile expressions, draw a wavy line. For no expressions, leave it blank.

Love means sacrificing for others. Would you be willing to give up some event you really cared about if it were important to one of your parents, brothers, or sisters that you do so?

_____

_____

Would others give up something important for you?

_____

_____

How much time do you spend together as a family each week?

_____

_____

Is this enough?

_____

_____

Draw another dining table, and this time, between each family member write or symbolize what kinds of sacrifice or serving are exchanged. For instance: Dad pays the bills. Sister helps her brother with his homework.

```
┌─────────────────────────────────────────────┐
│                                               │
│                                               │
│                                               │
│                                               │
│                                               │
│                                               │
│                                               │
│                                               │
└─────────────────────────────────────────────┘
```

Love is not based on what you do, but on who you are. Could you do anything so awful that your parents would never love you again?

_____

_____

Could they do anything that would make you totally cut
yourself off from them?

_____

_____

What do you think your parents hope you will be when you are
an adult?

_____

_____

What kind of person?

_____

Are their expectations positive?

_____

Do you feel that your parents' love for you depends on
meeting their expectations?

_____

_____

What about other family members?

_____

_____

Does your love for any family members depend on whether
they meet your expectations?

_____

_____

Do your parents supply your basic needs?

_____

_____

Does any member of your family seem to want to hurt or destroy another member? _____ First Corinthians 13 is the Bible's classic unsentimental statement of love. Here are the qualities described. Grade your family, A to F, on each quality:

patient _____   trusting _____

kind _____   hopeful _____

not envious _____   persevering _____

not boastful _____   protective _____

not proud _____   not rude _____

not easily angered _____   not self-seeking _____

keeps no record of wrongs _____

delighted with good, not evil _____

EVALUATION: It's fairly unusual for a family not to have love—though it does happen. More commonly, the love isn't expressed well, or isn't understood when it's expressed. For instance, your father may think of going to work as an act of love for you, but you have never understood how he feels about it. Or the love is conditional. You may love your parents providing they don't get tough about curfews.

As you look through your answers above, ask yourself, *Do my parents love me? Do the members of our family love each other?* Then ask, *How well do we communicate that love? Do we try to understand the unique ways each person expresses love?*

ACTION: If you see a basic lack of love in your family, check your evaluation by talking to an older friend of the family, a pastor, or a counselor. If there is no love, you can probably do very little at this point to stimulate it. You would be better off to accept its absence and look for love elsewhere.

If you feel love needs work, first ask, *Why isn't love better expressed, better understood? Can the causes be changed?* In some cases, you may never understand why love isn't better expressed. In other cases, understanding won't change anything immediately. A father who can't say "I love you" because *his* father could never say it won't learn how to say it instantly. But there can be gradual change.

You can never force someone to love you. But you can do two things:

1. You can express love to them. People usually fail to express love because they are insecure. When you practice letting them know you love them, they will probably begin to respond back.

2. You can let them know how you feel. Be sure you don't accuse; just describe your feelings, and how their actions look to you. This can be done in either a family council or in individual conversation. But be ready to hear how *they* feel about you.

COMMUNICATION

When you say something that is important to you, do you feel everyone in your family listens and tries to understand what you said?

_____

When they speak, do you listen and try to understand?

_____

_____

On the average, what percentage of conversation at your house is:

complaining _____   stimulating _____

encouraging _____   fun _____

small talk _____

Meals are important times for talking. Do you regularly have meals together?

_____

_____

Is there real conversation, or is the TV on?

_____

Is everyone in a hurry?

_____

_____

Does your family discuss important topics together?

_____

_____

Do you have a specific time set aside when these topics could surface?

_____

When you are feeling down and need someone to talk to, is there someone in your family you would feel free to open up to?

_____

_____

Do you think the same is true of other family members?

_____

For each family member, name the person he or she would be most likely to open up to.

_____

_____

EVALUATION: Checking your answers to the questions above, ask yourself, *Do we have trouble expressing feelings? Do we have trouble discussing stimulating and important subjects?* Then ask, *Are we just reluctant to open up? Or are there obstacles in the way we carry on family business—like we're always too busy, or the TV is always on?*

ACTION: Make a list of subjects you would like to see discussed and then think of two open-ended questions to ask about each subject.

Practice affirming what is said. Even if you don't agree, try to say something positive about what was said, how it was said, or the fact that it was said at all. If you don't understand, ask for an explanation.

In a family council, bring up the problem of communication. Perhaps you can agree to eat one meal a day together. Perhaps you can take time out from TV to talk, play, discuss a book or the day's news, play a game, or have a regular family council.

RESPECT

Freedom and respect go hand in hand. If your mother or father says something that you believe is totally out of touch with the real world, do you usually ridicule him or her?

_____

_____

_____

If you said something your family disagreed with, would they attack you or would they merely express their disagreement and begin a discussion?

_____

_____

_____

What qualities do you admire in your parents?

_____

_____

What qualities do you admire in your siblings?

_____

_____

Are there any qualities in you that family members tell you they admire?

_____

_____

Do you feel that when you reach the age of twenty-one your parents will be glad to let you live your own life?

_____

_____

Is each member of your family—parents included—encouraged in hobbies or other interests that are not necessarily shared by the rest of the family?

_____

_____

Do you have any privacy? _____ Where and when?

_____

_____

EVALUATION: As you consider your answers to the questions above, do you sense you are respected enough so you're allowed to think your own thoughts and form your own life? Do you respect your parents in the same way?

Do you think your family is geared toward gradually giving you independence, or do you see the family as trying to hold on to its members forever?

Is there admiration and respect for each other within your

family? (It's hard to give anyone freedom to be himself when you don't respect what he is.)

ACTION: You can't force anyone to respect you any more than you can force someone to love you. But you can *earn* respect; you can't *earn* love.

What would earn respect in your family? Getting good grades? Being more cheerful? Sticking to your curfew? As long as it's something positive and achievable, set out to do it, without making a big deal of it.

Are there specific areas in which you don't feel respected? Talk privately to the people involved about how that lack of respect makes you feel. Ask how you can earn respect in that area.

It's hard to respect someone who doesn't respect you. Develop a strategy for communicating respect for the way your parents have chosen to live. This will involve asking them questions about their choices so that you understand them. It will also involve verbally communicating respect for them as persons, even when you don't think you would make the same choices.

WHOLENESS

Is there any member of your family—especially a parent—who is consistently jumpy, nervous, or antagonistic?

_____

_____

Does any member of your family frequently withdraw or stay out of conversations or activities?

_____

_____

Is anyone in your family frequently sick?

_____

_____

Does any member of your family complain a great deal?

_____

_____

Is any member of your family always too busy to talk?

_____

_____

Does any member of your family lack close friends he or she can talk to about his or her feelings?

_____

_____

Is any member of your family constantly in trouble? Drunk or on drugs? Fighting? Losing jobs?

_____

_____

Do your parents seem to fight and disagree frequently?

_____

_____

Is any member of your family constantly tired?

_____

_____

EVALUATION: If you answered yes to any of the above questions, it could be your family's problems stem from this area. It is hard for someone to function as a good parent, brother, or sister if he or she doesn't feel capable of functioning as a human being. Any real improvement in your family has to involve accepting the fact that he or she has trouble living as a whole person, and then finding a way to help.

Wholeness also means that a family should work together in unity. If one or more family members live on the fringes, they need to be brought in.

ACTION: Talk to the person you think is having trouble. Ask questions to find out how he or she is really feeling and to learn how you can be more supportive.

If the person really seems troubled, check your evaluation with someone else. Talk to the other parent or to a pastor or a counselor whom you trust.

Make up your mind to accept less-than-perfect behavior from the person who seems to be having trouble. Encourage that person to get professional counseling.

With other family members, discuss how the troubled or excluded member can be brought into the center of the family. This may mean spending more time at home.

DISCIPLINE

At your house, are chores shared relatively equally, or do some members do most of the work? List the household chores and who does each one.

_____

_____

_____

_____

_____

_____

Make a complete list of the rules in your family.

_____

_____

_____

_____

_____

_____

Are the rules clear and well understood? _____ Do your parents apply the rules fairly and consistently?

_____

_____

Do you feel that your parents listen to you and are willing to consider your opinion before telling you what to do?

_____

_____

Do you feel that over time you are learning more how to think for yourself and make your own decisions?

_____

_____

How disciplined are you? List areas of your life requiring discipline (i.e. sports, homework, dating), and grade yourself on discipline in each area.

_____

_____

_____

_____

EVALUATION: Referring to the questions above, try to decide whether you are underruled or overruled. Also ask, *Is the point of each rule clear? Do I understand how it may help get necessary work done, or help keep me safe, or help me grow more mature?*

ACTION: Consider asking for a family council to discuss specific rules. Write out the rules as you understand them, then discuss them with your parents to make sure you understand.

Ask for help in disciplining your life (homework, getting enough sleep, getting to school on time, etc.) if you think it's needed.

Ask for a merit system, wherein you can earn certain freedoms if you act responsibly. For instance: Can you stay out late one night a month if you make it in on time the other nights?

FAITH

Does your family share faith in Jesus Christ?

_____

_____

Is God a daily source of strength to your family?

_____

_____

Do you go to church together?

_____

_____

Religiously, do you feel your parents are most concerned with what you *do* (go to church, pray, not swear or drink) or what you *are?*

_____

_____

Can you treat your parents not as people who should be perfect but as human beings who can make mistakes?

_____

_____

EVALUATION: Does your family have faith at all? Or does faith need to be further developed and expressed? If the latter, where do you see a need for growth?

ACTION: In a family, a "witness" can't be effective with just words. If you don't act in a helpful, loving manner, your parents will never accept your faith.

Don't let your faith be in conflict with family loyalty if you can avoid it. Do go to church regularly, even if your family doesn't; but don't insist that your family's church is worthless or that you can never go to family events because there's a prayer meeting somewhere.

Obey family rules as much as you can, and communicate as much as you can with your family, even if you don't always get a response. Don't preach or make a long speech; just tell what you are thinking and feeling, both positive and negative.

If possible, ask for a family council where everyone is encouraged to talk about what he believes and in what areas he wishes he had more faith. Don't argue; affirm whatever is good and keep your mouth shut the rest of the time. Otherwise you'll sound self-righteous to your family, whether you are or not.

If possible, suggest that your family establish a time to pray together for each other.

Most importantly, move closer to God yourself. If your faith is helping you, your family will eventually realize it, and maybe even learn from it.